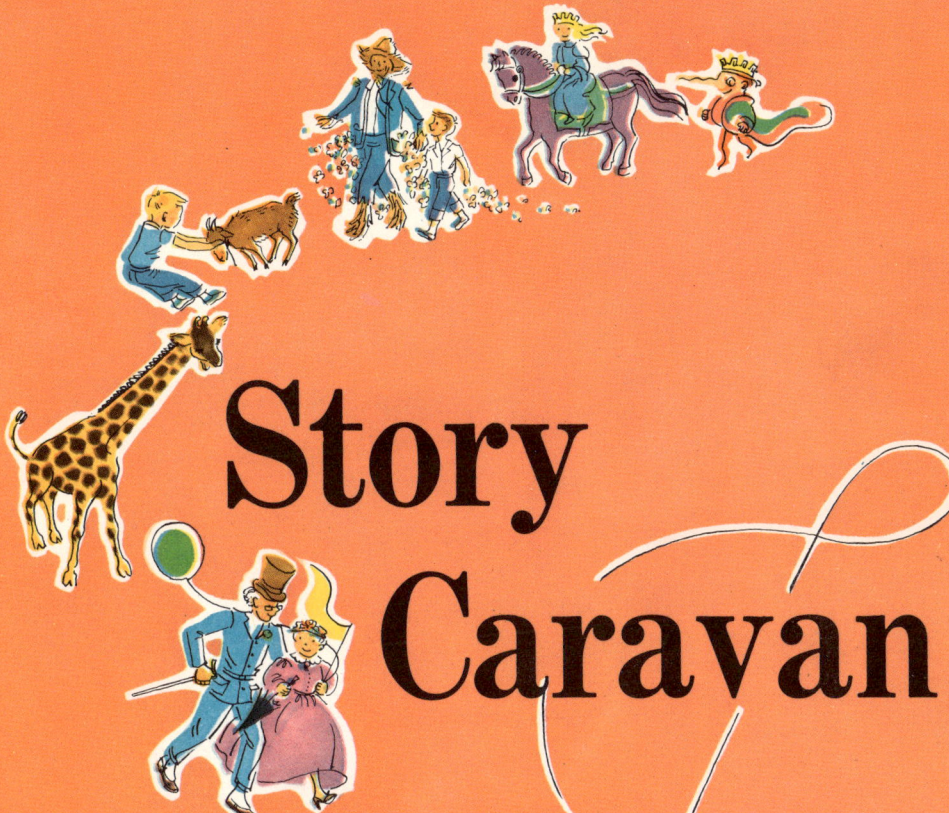

Story Caravan

by

William D. Sheldon
Mary C. Austin

1961

ALLYN AND BACON, INC.

Boston   New York   Chicago
Atlanta   Dallas   San Francisco

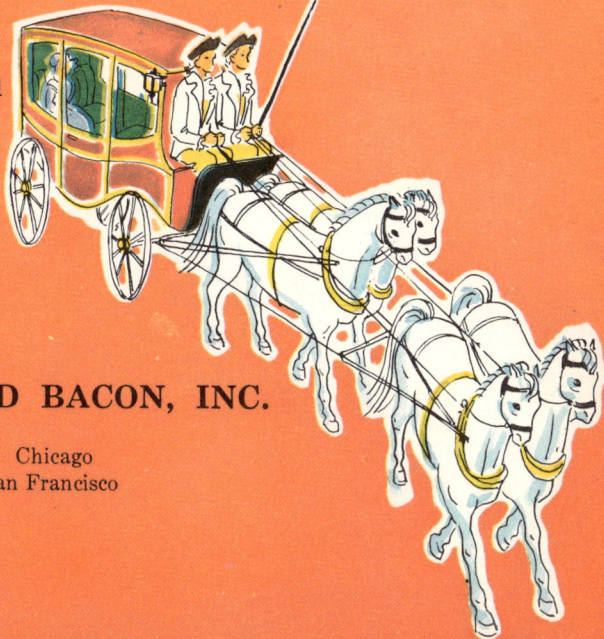

SHELDON BASIC READING SERIES

STORY CARAVAN

Illustrated
by

ALBERT JOUSSET
CHESLIE D'ANDREA
BERYL BAILEY-JONES
GERTRUDE ELLIOTT ESPENSCHEID

Acknowledgment for permission to use or adapt other than original selections in this book is given on page 272 or at the bottom of the page on which the selection begins.

Contents

Just for Fun

Eddie's Adventures

The End of the Rainbow

Stories
of Long Ago

The Peddler's Clock

Mother Wants a Clock

Miles, Jim, and Timothy Bell needed no clock to tell them when it was time to bring the cows home. It would have done them no good to wish for one either. Father did not want a clock in the house. He was too proud of the big silver watch which his own father had bought many years ago.

Father did not carry his watch every day because he did not want anything to happen to it. A few times he had let the children hold it. When he went to church or away on a journey, he usually wore the watch. He never wore it any other time.

But Father did not go away often. Most of the time the watch lay in its large case. This was in the tall desk in the farmhouse where the Bells lived in 1882.

So the family told time by the sun in the sky. When the sun was at a certain place, Timothy knew that it was time for him and his brothers to bring Betsy, Suzie, and Muley home to milk.

Miles, who was the youngest, said that Betsy was his cow. Jim pretended that Suzie belonged to him. Muley, a gentle cow without horns, was Timothy's pet. Each boy milked his own cow, morning and night. Then they carried in the full milk pails for the Bell family's use.

7

Mother had been a little angry with Father on the day that he had bought Muley. "Another cow!" she exclaimed. "When Betsy and Suzie give us all the milk we need? I do believe, Jonathan, you have no sense about cows. I wish that you had bought us a clock instead of another cow."

Father said, "We have one very good timepiece in the house. That's enough. Besides, a clock is just an ornament!"

"Now, Jonathan," said Grandmother Bell, "a clock is certainly more than an ornament. Elizabeth wants a clock in a case with pictures painted on the glass."

"That is a silly wish, Elizabeth," said Father. "Clocks are expensive, and I can't buy one."

"But, Father," said Prudence, "those new shelf-clocks with wooden works are not very expensive."

"A clock would be company," Mother said softly. At that everyone laughed, for Mother was never without company, with the house full of children. Sometimes there were visitors, too.

Father was kind, but he was also the master of his house. "We shall have no clock," he said.

So Mother had to do without a clock, and Muley stayed on the farm.

Mother's Bargain

One summer morning a few weeks later, Father started very early for the village on business. He was dressed in his best clothes with his silver watch in his pocket.

It always seemed strange on the farm when Father was away on business. The days seemed longer, and the nights were still and lonely.

That evening when supper was almost ready, the family heard someone outside. Everyone crowded into the doorway. A tall, thin man with long whiskers was getting off his horse.

"Perhaps it's a visitor," said Miles.

"A peddler, I think," said Mother.

10

"Good day to you," the peddler said to Mother. "And to all who live in this house," he added. He took his large bag off the horse and laid it down on the grass. Carefully he took something out of his bag. There was — a clock.

"I come from Ebenezer Plump's shop," said the peddler. "I am almost at my journey's end. I have sold every watch, every candlestick, every clock, and every expensive ornament that I had when I left the shop a week ago. All have been sold, good woman, but this shelf-clock and three cowbells. What will you give me for this fine clock?"

He laid the clock in Mother's arms.
Mother smiled as she looked down at it.
It was just the clock she had wanted! It
was in a beautiful case with little pink roses
painted on the glass.

"Just set it up in the house somewhere,"
said the peddler, "and I will start it going.
Then you can hear its cheerful notes when
it strikes the hour."

Mother stood it on the shelf in the kitchen.
Soon they could hear the clock.

"Now," said the peddler, "when the
minute-hand points to twelve, and the
hour-hand to twelve, the clock will strike
the hour."

12

Timothy held his breath, waiting, while the minute-hand moved. Sure enough, when it pointed to twelve, they heard twelve cheerful notes. Everyone looked at Mother. She stood looking at the clock. Her face was pink and her eyes were bright.

"Now," said the peddler, "let me set it for you."

"Oh, no!" said Mother, "I have no money, and Mr. Bell is not home." She turned her back to the clock and looked at the peddler with tears in her eyes. "You had better take the clock away," she said.

It really made everyone feel sad to see Mother. She was giving up the beautiful clock with little pink roses painted on its glass.

"Oh, Mother!" cried Prudence. "Maybe the man would trade something for the clock."

"What have you to trade?" asked the peddler.

Mother looked at Prudence. She looked at Grandmother. She held a corner of her apron to her mouth as she thought. Then she threw back her head. She spoke softly, "I have a cow."

"Elizabeth!" exclaimed Grandmother.

"Mother!" exclaimed Prudence.

"Mother! Which cow?" Timothy's voice sounded frightened.

But Mother looked straight at the peddler. "Are you interested in such a trade?" she asked.

"I'm interested, if it's a good cow."

"We have only good cattle," said Mother. "Come, you may see for yourself." She led the way down the path to the barn. Timothy ran after her. Miles also started to run after them, but Mother turned quickly. "Go back into the house, children," she said. "This bargain is between me and the peddler."

Timothy stood by the window. He caught his breath as Mother and the peddler came out of the barn. The peddler was leading Muley!

"Oh-h-h, Grandmother," said Timothy with tears in his eyes, "he's taking my cow!"

Grandmother caught him just as he was running out of the door. "Timothy! Do not say a word. Muley is not really your cow. Your mother is doing what she thinks best."

There was the peddler going off down the dusty road with his horse and Muley.

"Now we'll have supper," said Mother.

"How can she do this?" thought Timothy. Off he ran after the peddler, who heard him and waited. Timothy looked up at him. "You don't even know her name," he cried. "It's Muley."

"I might have guessed," laughed the peddler, "since she hasn't any horns. That's one reason I wanted her."

16

Timothy dug his toes into the dusty road. "You — you'll be good to her, won't you?"

"She will be Ebenezer Plump's cow, not mine. But don't be afraid. The master will be good to her."

"Let me pet her just once," cried Timothy. He leaned against the cow and patted her neck. "Good-by, Muley," he whispered.

"I guess you feel sad to see her go," said the peddler. "Here, I'll give you a present." He dug into his bag and pulled out the three cowbells. He leaned down from his horse and gave them to Timothy.

"Thank you," said Timothy. For a moment he felt happy about the present. But as the peddler disappeared, Timothy thought, "Three cowbells for only two cows!"

Still, the evening seemed gay. The new clock on the shelf was like having a cheerful visitor in the house. The eyes of everyone were always turning to look at it. They watched the minute-hand as it traveled around. They saw the slow-moving hour-hand. The clock made the big, plain kitchen seem beautiful.

Father's Bargain

But the next morning there was no Muley to milk. Timothy felt lost without his job. As the hour of Father's return came nearer, the family grew quiet. They looked at each other and at Mother's mouth. It became straighter and straighter.

It was late afternoon when Father returned. He was happy to be in his pleasant home again. He put his watch carefully away in its case in the tall desk. He changed his clothes, and the family all sat down to supper in the kitchen.

"There isn't anyone who can cook as well as you can, Elizabeth," he said. He was just about to take a great bite of turkey when the clock struck six cheerful notes. He looked up quickly.

"What's that?" he asked.

"That's the new clock, Jonathan," said Grandmother. "Doesn't it sound nice?"

Father looked at the clock. "Where did it come from?"

"I got it from a peddler," answered Mother.

"And what did you give him for it?" asked Father.

"One of the cows," said Mother. "Muley."

Father pushed back his chair and looked at Mother. "You — you mean you traded Muley for that ornament?"

"Yes," said Mother.

Father's face was like a thundercloud. He stood up. "I won't say what I think. The children — " and he walked out of the house toward the barn with long, fast steps.

It was an unhappy evening. Everyone went to bed very early.

The next day was rainy. At breakfast Father said, "Since there is no cow for you to milk, Timothy, you may come and help me in the barn."

In the barn Timothy said, "Father, I thought it was a bad piece of bargaining, too. The cow's worth lots more than the clock."

Father patted him on the head. "You must not say unkind things about your mother, Timothy."

"No, Father," answered Timothy. "I do think the clock is nice. But, Father, I want to tell you. Last night in bed I planned how we can get Muley back. I could go to work for Ebenezer Plump until I can pay for her."

"That would take a long time, Son," said Father. He gave Timothy a look that made the boy's heart pound with happiness. They worked quietly for a few moments longer. Then Father spoke again. "Son, run to the house and bring me my coat and hat and gloves."

After Father had washed his hands and put on his hat, coat, and gloves, he brought out his horse. "Now, Timothy, I'm going away on business. You can say I shall be back by evening." And Father rode off in the rain and the mud.

22

All day Timothy wondered where Father had gone. Mother looked worried.

The new bells that Betsy and Suzie wore made a pleasant noise as the cows came across the field that evening. The rain had stopped, and there was a rainbow in the sky. Timothy was standing by the barn watching it. He dug his toes into the soft mud. Suddenly he saw Father coming down the road with Muley.

"Here, Timothy," he said. "Here's your cow! Take her into the barn where she belongs."

"Father!" cried Timothy. "How did you get her back?"

"I went to Ebenezer Plump's shop and paid the man what the clock was worth."

Father ate a big supper that evening. He got up from the table and stretched.

Then he said, "That's a handsome clock, Elizabeth, very handsome! It wasn't very expensive either. Next winter I will build you a new shelf for it. How would you like that?"

"I'd like it very much, Jonathan."

Mother and Father smiled at each other. Suddenly it seemed as if the whole house were filled with sunshine. The children began to laugh and chatter. Grandmother's face was full of happiness.

Timothy was happiest of all. He took the pail and ran out to the barn. First he tied the bell around Muley's neck. "Three bells — three cows," he said. Then he sat down to milk his cow.

The Little Cook

A Kind Act

Betty lived many, many years ago. She was not very big, but she had learned to help her mother.

She could wash the dishes and help keep the house clean. But best of all, she liked to cook.

One day Betty was alone at home. Her father and mother and brother had gone to town to see a great sight.

President Washington was making a journey through the country. He was going from town to town in a fine coach pulled by a team of six white horses.

Four soldiers rode in front of the coach, Betty's mother had told her, and four others rode behind it. They were all dressed in white and gold.

At every town crowds of people waited to see the President. Little girls threw flowers before him as he drove past. Little boys, dressed like soldiers, marched to band music to meet him. Betty's brother Jack was to be one of these boys today.

But Betty could not see this wonderful sight. Someone had to stay at home to look after the house.

"I will stay at home and cook supper for you," Betty had said. "Jack must march with the boys to meet the President."

"You are a good girl, Betty," said her mother. "You know where we keep the meat and the butter and the cream."

Betty felt sad that morning as her parents rode away quite early. She did want to see George Washington, the first President of her country.

Betty Gets Her Wish

By seven o'clock Betty's work was finished. She sat on the front porch and watched the people going to town.

"Oh, if I could only see the President!" she said to herself.

But what sound was that? Someone was coming! Perhaps she would have visitors.

In the clear April morning four soldiers were riding along the dusty road. Behind them came a great white coach pulled by a team of six white horses.

Betty jumped up, for they all stopped in front of the house. She was going to have visitors that April morning.

A tall man stepped from the coach and came up the path to the porch. He took off his hat as he reached the steps.

"Good morning," said the tall man. "Can you give me some breakfast?"

"I'll try, sir," said Betty respectfully. "My parents have taken my brother Jack to town to see the great George Washington. I am all alone here with no one to help me."

"If you are as quick as you are pretty, you won't need any help," said the man. "Just get a good breakfast for me, and you shall see Washington before your brother does."

Betty almost danced with happiness. "I will do the best I can, sir," she said respectfully.

Quickly she put on a clean apron. Then she spread a white cloth on the dining room table. She set out the best dishes and silver on the white cloth.

Betty brought some roast chicken and honey and bread from the kitchen shelf. She ran to the cellar for butter to spread on the bread.

She put some fresh eggs from the cellar into hot water and cut pieces of the roast chicken. When everything was ready, she called the hungry man to the dining room.

He had a fine breakfast. As the tall man left the table, he smiled and leaning over, kissed Betty's forehead.

"Now, my pretty little cook," he said, "you may tell your brother Jack that you saw Washington before he did. Tell him he kissed you, too, for I am George Washington."

The Saving Sneeze

An Adventure in the Woods

Mary thought she hadn't done anything wonderful that Saturday morning. She had only wanted to save the young American soldier.

Even after it was all over she didn't understand why mother had kissed her on the forehead and cried about what had happened. Mother had told Father about it that night. Father had put his hand on her shoulder and said, "You're a brave little girl."

It all happened a long time ago. Mary lived with her parents and her grandmother in a log cabin. They were miles away from the main roads. Very little news of the war between the Americans and the British came to them.

Sometimes they heard the far-off sound of a drum and marching feet. Other times Mary saw the red coats of the British soldiers through the trees or the dark clothes of the American soldiers going by.

But always when she saw them, she would hide in the bushes carefully. Then, when the soldiers had passed by, she would run home as fast as she could.

Mary's playground was the forest around the clearing where their log cabin stood. It was a wonderful playground of bright flowers, singing birds, and little forest animals. A stream ran through the woods. Mary liked to make little boats to float on the water.

Mary's best friend was her rag doll, Becky. Grandmother had made Becky for her birthday. Wherever Mary went, Becky went, too. They had many secret adventures together in the woods.

One Saturday Mary and Becky were playing near the stream. Mary was making a boat to sail on the water as she talked to her rag doll.

Suddenly she stopped. She turned her head and listened. From far off came the sound of a drum and marching feet. Louder and clearer still came the sound of gunfire. What was it? Could it be a battle? Mary gathered Becky closer in her arms. She was too afraid to run home.

"S-s-sh," she whispered to her doll. "Be very still. They must be soldiers fighting a battle. We must not let them see us."

Mary and Becky hid in some bushes until the sound of marching feet passed. Then Mary took a deep breath.

Help for a Friend

Mary placed her little boat in the water and walked beside it as it sailed along. She didn't know how far she had gone when she saw something red on the ground. She stopped suddenly. There was something lying in the bushes just ahead!

Mary decided to run home. But she saw that the thing did not move, so she went a few steps nearer. There, lying face down on the ground, was a young American soldier. His coat and shirt were tattered, and his head was cut.

"Oh!" cried Mary.

At the sound of her voice the soldier turned his head and tried to get up. But he fell back. He looked up at her with such frightened eyes that Mary was not afraid of him.

"What's the trouble?" she asked.

"Don't tell them I'm here!" whispered the soldier. "Don't let them get me!"

"There's no one here," said Mary. "Only Becky and me. Who wants you?"

"The British soldiers caught me. I ran away. But they will come back and shoot me."

"Oh, they can't do that!" Mary cried. "Come home with me. My mother is a good nurse. She and Grandmother will find some way to save you."

Mary helped him to his feet. He leaned on her shoulder. They started slowly along the trail to the log cabin.

Mary's mother was standing in the doorway. She ran quickly to meet them.

"What is it? What has happened?"

"The British want to shoot him!" cried
Mary.

"Bring him into the cabin," Mary's
mother said. "Whatever he has done, he
is hurt and needs our help."

Mother shut the door and put the young
American in Grandmother's high-backed
rocking chair. Then Mother washed the
soldier's face and took care of his head.
Grandmother gave him a clean shirt and
sewed up his tattered coat. Then they
gave him some water to drink.

Grandmother spoke. "Now tell us all
about it."

The young soldier tried to get up. "I must go now," he said. "You have been very kind, but I do not want to get you into trouble. The British must not find me here."

Grandmother put out her hand. "Sit still," she said. "Tell us the trouble."

"I was with a scouting party," the young soldier explained. "Somehow I got lost from the others in the scouting party. Then the Redcoats caught me. They tried to shoot me, but I got away and hid in the bushes."

"Don't worry, lad," Grandmother spoke gently. "We shall do what we can."

The Search

"Quiet!" cried Mother suddenly. "I hear voices. We must speak no untruth, but we will try to give the scout protection. Where can we put him?"

"Here," said Grandmother. "Get in the bed, under the feather bed, quickly!"

In a moment the frightened lad was hidden under the feather bed.

"Look!" Mary pointed out. "The feather bed sticks up too much. They might guess that he is here!"

"So they might," said Grandmother. "Mary, lie down on this side of the bed. Pull up the blanket!"

Grandmother was sewing, and Mother was standing by her spinning wheel when the soldiers came to the door.

"We are looking for a runaway soldier," said the captain. "Has he come here?"

"Come in and look."

The soldiers stepped in, shutting the door behind them. They looked around the room and saw Grandmother sewing.

"Have you searched the woods?" asked Mother, still busy at her spinning wheel.

Suddenly a terrible thing happened. As the men turned away, the hidden soldier sneezed!

The soldier at the door turned around quickly. "What was that?" he shouted.

Mary's heart stood still. Quick as could be, she pulled the blanket over her face and sneezed. It sounded like the first sneeze.

"Oh, it's you!" laughed the soldier. He looked at her for a moment. "This little girl is ill. Her face is as red as fire. She needs looking after. I know I have children of my own."

"I'm a nurse," said Mother. "I'll look after her."

"Yes," said the soldier. "I think you will." He turned and disappeared with the other men.

The two women rushed to help the young soldier out from under the feather bed. He couldn't seem to say "Thank you" often enough to Mary.

But Mary couldn't see why it was so wonderful. She and Becky had just as exciting adventures in the woods almost every day!

Stories of Make-Believe

Otherwise

There must be magic,
Otherwise,
How could day turn to night,

And how could sailboats,
Otherwise,
Go sailing out of sight,

And how could peanuts,
Otherwise,
Be covered up so tight?

Aileen Fisher

The Real Princess

A Knock at the Gate

Once upon a time there was a prince who wanted to marry a princess. But he wanted a **real** princess. He traveled all over the world to find one. Nowhere could he find the one he wanted to marry.

There were princesses enough, but it was not easy to find out if they were real ones. There was always something about them that was not as it should be. So the sad prince came home again.

One evening in the spring there was a
terrible storm. There was thunder and
lightning, and the rain came down in
streams. Suddenly a knocking was heard
at the city gate. The old King himself went
to open it.

It was a princess who stood outside in
front of the gate. But, goodness me! What
a sight the rain and the wind had made her
look. The water streamed down from her
hair and her clothes. It ran down into
the toes of her shoes and out at the heels.
But she said that she was a real princess.

The Princess and the Pea

"Well, we shall soon see if that is an untruth," thought the old Queen, but she said nothing. She went into the bedroom, took all the bedding off the bed, and laid a pea on the bottom. Then she took twenty mattresses and laid them on the pea for protection. Then she piled twenty feather beds on top of the mattresses. This was where the princess had to lie all night. In the morning she was asked how she had slept.

"Oh, very badly!" said the princess. "I hardly closed my eyes all night. I haven't the least idea what was in the bed. It seemed to be an enormous rock. My whole body is black and blue from head to heels. Goodness me!"

Now they knew that she was a real princess. She had felt the pea through twenty mattresses and twenty feather beds. Nobody but a real princess could have such unusual skin.

So the prince took her for his wife. Now he knew that he had found a real princess to marry. And the pea was put in a glass case in the palace. It may still be seen there, at least if no one has taken it away.

The Purple Horse

The Unusual Wish

Marlaine was a poor, lonely little girl. She was busy from morning until night caring for her grandmother and their little house near the woods.

From their doorway Marlaine could look across the river valley and up a very high cliff. There she saw the beautiful castle of the King.

Often Marlaine stopped her work, looked up at the castle, and sighed, "I wish I lived in a beautiful castle. The little girl who lives there must be the happiest girl in all the world."

Nothing could be farther from the truth, however. The Princess who lived in the lovely castle at the top of the cliff was not at all happy. In fact, she was probably the most unhappy girl in the whole world.

The Princess could have anything she wanted. She needed only to ask her father, the King, and he would order it for her. At least this was what had happened until the day she asked for a purple horse.

The King heard his daughter's wish and almost ordered a purple horse for her. Suddenly he stopped.

"A purple horse!" he roared. "That is impossible!"

"But, Father, you have always said you would do anything to make me happy. I think a purple horse would be the most wonderful horse in all the world."

"Indeed it would be — ah, ah — different, dear. But why must you have a purple horse?"

"Purple horses are better than others. I just know they are. They must be because they're — well, they're purple," cried the Princess.

The King nodded, and an order was sent throughout the land. The order said that anyone who owned a purple horse must bring it to the castle at once.

Several weeks passed, but no one sent a purple horse for the Princess. No one had ever seen a purple horse.

The Princess became so unhappy that she fell ill. People shook their heads and sighed, "If only a purple horse could be found, but that's impossible!"

Finally the King promised a large reward to the owner of a purple horse. But nobody appeared, and the Princess grew weaker and weaker.

Marlaine's Idea

Marlaine stood in her doorway looking up at the castle. She was thinking of the Princess, for Marlaine knew how unhappy the Princess was. Marlaine thought, too, of the cloth a neighbor had asked her to dye. It would make a lovely dress. Marlaine wished she could dye her own dress such a lovely color.

Suddenly Marlaine had an idea. She rushed out to the barn and looked at Nell, the family horse. "It might work," she thought. "Anyway I'll try."

That evening and the next morning Marlaine worked and worked on Nell. She didn't tell anyone about her idea.

The following day Marlaine appeared at the castle and asked to see the King. At first the guards only laughed and stared. When they heard her reason, they rushed to tell the King.

The King did not wait for Marlaine to be brought in, but he quickly hurried out to meet her. He could hardly believe his eyes. He stared at the little girl with a purple horse. Of course the purple horse had a blanket spread over her back. However, when you looked closely, you could see that she was really purple.

The King was very happy. "Thank you. I want to reward you, Marlaine."

But Marlaine only smiled and said, "I do not want any reward. I only want our Princess to be well and happy with her purple horse."

Soon the Princess was well enough to ride her purple horse. People came from far and near to see the most wonderful horse in all the world. They shook their heads and whispered, "What a strange horse. She is surely the most wonderful horse in all the world because she is purple."

One day while the Princess was riding her purple horse, rain began to fall. There was a thunder and lightning storm. Both of them got very wet. When the Princess reached the castle, she left her horse at the gate and hurried inside.

The Purple Horse Is No Longer Purple

The next day the Princess dressed to go for a ride on the little horse she had come to love so well. The King rushed into her room shouting, "The purple horse is no longer purple! The purple horse is no longer purple!"

And indeed the horse was no longer purple. The rain had washed off the coat of purple-colored dye. There stood Marlaine's family horse, Nell.

The King was very angry. Finally however, he thought of Marlaine. He sent for his soldiers and roared, "Find the girl who fooled me. Find her and bring her here. I'll have her head for this trick!"

The soldiers rushed off to find Marlaine.

The King was so angry that he had been fooled that he did not notice the Princess' smile. She was used to hearing her father shout and roar. He didn't frighten her.

Much to the King's surprise, the Princess began to laugh. "Why," she said, "I love my little horse even if she isn't purple any more. She is so gentle and good. I shall remember the next time to choose a horse because she is a good horse and not to choose one by her color. I still think my little horse is the most wonderful horse in all the world. I hope the soldiers do find the little girl who brought me the horse. She should have the reward which you promised. She tried to give me a purple horse, and she helped to make me well again."

When the King heard these words, he stopped shouting and roaring. "Why, why, ah-h-h, you are right, my dear. The little girl did help to make you well. After all, I didn't ask for a horse that would stay purple forever."

"She was such a kind little girl. Do you think she would like to visit us here at the castle? It's often lonely living in such a big castle."

Marlaine was very happy to visit the Princess in the castle. Sometimes she and the Princess even took turns riding the most wonderful horse in all the world.

James the Huntsman

The Strange Little Man

Once upon a time there were two brothers named John and James. Their father had left them a house and garden. This was hardly enough for one, to say nothing of two! John, who was the older brother, decided he should have all of it.

James had to go out into the world and make his way as well as he could.

"I don't know what's to become of me," James cried to himself. "I should like to be a huntsman, but where can I find a horn, or a horse, or a hunting gun?"

And then he fell asleep. He got no more than twenty winks when suddenly he heard a little voice say, "Help me! Help me once, and I'll help you twice!"

James jumped up quickly. He thought he had been dreaming. Then that little voice rang out again, "Help me! Help me once, and I'll help you twice!" The voice was close to the earth this time. James looked down carefully at his feet. What should he see but a tiny little man no bigger than your finger.

"I'll help you if I can," replied James. "What is your trouble?"

"I am shut out of house and home," said the little man. "There is a cow standing right over my doorway, and do what I can, she won't move."

"Well, we'll soon take care of that," said
James. He ran over to the cow and chased
her away.

"That was a good deed," said the little
man. "If you'll come back tomorrow at
midnight, I'll promise to reward you."

"But I want nothing, sir," said James.
"A good deed is its own reward."

"But a good deed cooks no food for a
hungry man," answered the dwarf. "Do as
I say, and you will be glad." Then he took
a hop, skip, and a jump and was gone down
a hole in the ground as quick as a wink.

James' Reward

The next evening James returned to the hill. At twelve, a strange thing happened. The hill rose up, high enough for James to walk under, and there in the middle stood the little dwarf.

"Come into my father's castle," said the dwarf. Then the hill closed round them, and James found himself inside a handsome palace. The floors were silver, the walls were gold, and the lights were diamonds shining like stars.

"Well!" said the little man. "Have you decided what will be your reward?"

"Yes," said James. He asked not for money nor food, but for the three things nearest and dearest to him — a horn, a horse, and a hunting gun.

"No sooner asked than done," said the dwarf, and he led James into a great cellar. It was filled from top to bottom with nothing but guns. There were guns big as trees and small as toothpicks, guns of gold and silver, and guns never seen by any other man on earth.

James looked at everything. Then he walked over to a far corner where there hung a rusty old gun. "This rusty old gun is good enough for me," he said.

"Very well," said the dwarf. "Choose the rusty gun, and may it serve you well."

Then they went on to a room filled with horns, horns tall as a man and small as toothpicks and some covered with diamonds. "Well," said James, as he took a long look around. His eyes rested on a plain little horn that had been thrown into a far corner. "That little horn is just the one for me."

"Very well," said the dwarf to James. "Choose your plain little horn, and may it play well."

And then the little man led James to a great barn where there were the finest horses you ever laid eyes on. Some you've never seen, too, horses with flapping wings, and horses with bright eyes and feet of fire. But there was one little gray animal. This one James decided to choose. "He is just right," James said. "He goes well with my old horn, that was thrown into a corner, and my rusty hunting gun."

"Very well," said the little man. "Take your plain little horse, and may you ride him well." Then there was a loud noise, and James found himself no longer in the rich palace barns but outside on the cold, dark hillside. He would have thought it all a dream, but there beside him stood the little horse, and in his hand were the horn and the hunting gun.

A Visit to the King

Now James was a huntsman at last. He got on the horse, and away he rode toward the King's palace. At the gates he was stopped by the guard. "What is your wish at the King's palace?" asked the guard.

"I wish a place with the King's huntsmen," replied James.

The guard stared at James and his rusty gun and old horn. Then he laughed and said, "Well, you'll wish long and late, my lad. But try if you must. You'll find the head huntsman over at the palace door near the tower."

"Thank you," said James. He passed some trees on the palace grounds. He saw a bird no bigger than a toothpick which lighted on his arm.

"Listen, listen," sang the little bird as he flapped his wings. "You carry a magic horn and hunting gun. Whenever you blow your horn, all who hear it must dance. Wherever you point your gun, all bears and deer will be killed."

"In this way you can serve the King," sang the little bird. "Now listen closely. The King's daughter and the Prince she was to marry were taken a long time ago by the king of the dwarfs. They were carried away to the very hill where you were last night. If you can free them and return them safely to the protection of the King, you will be a rich huntsman. The King will give you half of his country, too."

"Well," said James, "I'll do what I can, but I don't want half of the country."

"Thank you," said the little bird. "And may you win well." Then up he flew back into the trees.

James rode on to the tower until he reached the head huntsman. He said, "I wish to have a place with the King's huntsmen."

The head huntsman looked him up, and he looked him down. He slapped his knee and said with a laugh, "Well, you'll look high and low, and long and late before you find a place with the King's huntsmen." Off he rode, leaving poor James.

A moment later who should arrive but the King himself! The King asked, "What is your wish, young man?"

"I wish to be one of your huntsmen," said James. "And I wish to bring back your daughter and the Prince from the dwarf king."

"What strange wishes you have!" cried the King. "Do you not know that my daughter was taken away many years ago, and that I have not seen her since? Surely a poor lad like you could never find her."

"I have a horse, a magic horn, and a magic hunting gun," said James. "If you but follow me to the dwarf king's hill, I can show you."

A Visit to the Dwarf King

"Very well," said the King. "Your eyes are kind, and your hands are strong. I can see that you are not just talking."

The two of them set out on their horses for the dwarf king's palace. They arrived at the hill close to midnight. James stopped at the foot of the hill and said, "First we must call out the dwarf king." Then he blew on his horn for the first time a high sharp note.

As soon as the sharp note died away, there was a fearful noise from within the hill. Slowly it rose as before, and inside a rich palace shining like the sun they saw the dwarf king. He was a fearful-looking little man. He was no taller than your boot, with a nose as long as your arm, and eyes the size of plates. At the sight of James and the King on their horses the dwarf began to cry sadly.

"It's little use crying will do you," said
James. "It is the King's daughter you
must give up and all safe, too."

At this the dwarf king cried louder than
ever. "Gold and silver you may have," he
cried, "but not the King's young daughter.
She sings as sweetly as a bird from morning
until night, and I'll not give her up."

"Well," said James, "we'll see about that," and once more he raised the horn to his lips. This time he played a lively song made for dancing.

It set the dwarf to kicking his feet and spinning round and round, until he was out of breath and his legs were tired. Then over he fell on the point of his nose, and round and round he went again. Finally he cried, "Stop, stop! I am a very old man. You are shaking me to dust."

"Will you return my daughter as young and fair as when you took her?" cried the King.

"Younger and fairer," shouted the dwarf. So James stopped his lively song. The queer little man rushed to the back of the palace and returned a moment later with the lovely princess.

"But what of the young prince? Where is the Prince? Has he died?" cried James. "Up with him quickly, or you shall dance on your nose again."

"That is impossible! He is no longer here," said the dwarf king. James put his horn to his lips again. At that moment there was a soft noise, and looking up the Princess saw the little gray horse beside James.

"There is the Prince," she cried. "He was changed into a horse, so we could not run away together."

"Change him back into a man," cried the King.

"I will do as you ask if you will return my gun and horn," said the dwarf.

"Take them and gladly," exclaimed James as he gave them to the dwarf. The horse disappeared, and there before them stood the handsome young prince. Suddenly the mountain closed. The four happy people were standing in a valley far away from the dwarf's mountain.

"Well," said the King to James, "you have kept your promise, so I will keep mine. You shall own half my country, be a prince, and have your own crown and palace, too."

"I do not need much to be happy," said James. "I am only a poor man's son."

"You needn't have much to wear a crown and to live in a palace. Just keep your shoulders back and your head up."

And so there was nothing for James to do but to become a prince. And everyone lived happily ever after.

Holiday Stories

Valentines for America

Anya Learns about Valentines

Anya could hardly wait to get home from school to tell Mama all about the valentines. But for a minute she stood at the turn in the road to look at the house where she and Mama and Papa lived. To everybody else it might look like nothing but an old gray frame house. To Anya it was the most beautiful house in the world.

America, thought Anya, was wonderful, even if the children at school sometimes laughed at her. Before long they would not laugh. She would do everything the American way. Anya was going to start right now with the valentines.

"Mama!" Anya hurried into the house and put her schoolbooks carefully on the table. "Mama, could Papa take me to town in the truck to buy valentines?"

There was no answer. The kitchen was empty. On the table Anya found a note saying that Mama had gone with Papa to take the Campbells' pigs to market. Mama went whenever she could because she got lonesome.

"She's different, too," thought Anya, "and doesn't speak American very well." A sad thought struck her. "Oh, the valentines!"

The valentine box, gay with red and white paper, had been a great surprise to Anya. Miss Riggs, her teacher, had brought it into the school this morning. By listening to the chatter of the others and by looking at the February calendar, Anya learned that tomorrow would be Valentine's Day. Everybody would bring valentines to school. They would push them through the opening in the top of the box.

Anya had stood by her teacher after school. "Where do you buy them, please, Miss Riggs?"

"At the ten-cent store in town, Anya," Miss Riggs had said kindly. "A penny apiece, most of them. Or you can make pretty ones of your own out of red paper. They're fun to make."

"Yes, Miss Riggs. Thank you, please."

The children had laughed, and Anya's face had turned bright pink. It was so hard to remember not to say thank you and please both at once. But she had found out where to buy valentines.

"Should I buy one for everybody in the room?" Anya asked Frank, the friendly bus driver.

"If you want to," said Frank. "If you don't want to, you don't need to. Do what you please. It's a free country."

"Better if I do buy for all," Anya decided. "Even for the ones who laugh. They teach me what I do wrong, so I don't do it again."

Anya Is Disappointed

But now, sitting in the empty kitchen, Anya felt that everything would be wrong tomorrow. She was so disappointed that tears came into her eyes. If she had nothing to put in the box, the children would think she didn't like American ways.

"Perhaps I could walk to town," Anya thought, but a look at the clock told her she could not. It was six miles to town and, as Papa always said, seven miles back. The ten-cent store would be closed before Anya could get there.

"I could try to make some valentines the way Miss Riggs said." The trouble was that she had no red paper — in fact, none at all but her yellow school paper.

Anya poured herself a glass of milk and spread herself a piece of homemade bread with Mama's good butter. Then she sat down to think.

Mama said that food made everything look brighter. "Plain food is nice, but pretty food is twice as good."

Mama's cakes and cookies were always decorated on birthdays with little roses and the names of people. At Christmas a beautiful red Santa Claus was done in icing.

Anya fixed herself another piece of bread and butter and poured more milk.

"Christmas wrappings!" she thought suddenly. "Maybe some of the plain red paper will do." She hunted for it.

Mama was too neat. The plain red wrapping paper had already been put away, and none was left. Anya went back to her bread and butter.

Anya had supper ready when her parents arrived. They were rubbing their hands because it was a cold winter day.

Mama sniffed happily. "Smells good."

"Mama thinks the best thing about America is food," Papa said.

"Second best maybe," said Mama. "First is doing what you please."

"That's what Frank said." Anya set the hot vegetables, the meat, and the dessert on the table. "Papa, I have an American thing to do before tomorrow and nothing with which to do it."

Anya's father looked at the February calendar and smiled. "Nothing?" he asked. "Maybe you should think harder."

Mama cut the big chocolate cake which she had baked that morning for dessert. It was decorated with beautiful green leaves.

"It's too pretty to eat," said Anya.

But she was not thinking about the freshly baked chocolate cake. Her thoughts wandered upstairs and downstairs all over the house, but she found nothing to use for valentines. Her thoughts went downstairs to the cellar and back upstairs to the kitchen again.

"Papa!" cried Anya suddenly. "I thought harder."

Anya's Valentines

The next morning Anya got on the bus. She carried a large package neatly wrapped in brown paper and tied with string.

"What's in it?" everybody asked.

"Valentines," Anya answered proudly.

"Must be big ones," a child said.

"Probably they won't even go into the valentine box."

Anya said nothing. Even if her valentines were not like American ones, they were the best she could do. Anyway, Frank had certainly said, "Do as you please. It's a free country."

Anya marched into school and handed the package to Miss Riggs.

"Are those your valentines, Anya? Put them in the valentine box, please."

"They won't go in the box." Anya could feel her face getting red. "Will you open them for me?"

Miss Riggs opened Anya's package. The children crowded around as she lifted out large cookies decorated in red with white around the outside. In the middle of each cookie, Mama had put a name in white icing. She had baked a cookie for every child in the room.

Miss Riggs smiled at Anya as she called out the names. "You must tell your mother and father how glad we are to have such fine new Americans in our country."

Tears of happiness came into Anya's eyes. "Oh, thank you, please," she said.

But none of the children laughed this time. They were much too busy eating Anya's valentines for America.

Archie and the April Fools

A Hungry Visitor

"Ted," said Jim Butterfield, coming into the living room suddenly, "I don't like to say this, but there's a giraffe in the back yard."

His brother looked up from his camera, gave Jim a strange look, then eyed the calendar. The smile on his face grew wider. The calendar had told him the fact that it was April first.

"Run away, don't bother me," said Ted. "I'm busy. You know, Jim, light must be getting into our camera. We must get a new one as soon as we have enough money."

"We're going to get a projector," Jim said. "I don't like to say it again, but there is a giraffe in our back yard."

"I know, I know. There's a baby alligator in the kitchen, too, but don't bother me with that now. Just forget April Fool's Day." Ted sighed. "What kind of camera do you think we should get?"

"Projector," said Jim, looking thoughtfully out the window. "I take it all back. There isn't a giraffe in the back yard."

Ted said, "That's better. You can't catch me on those old April Fool jokes."

"He isn't in the back yard," said Jim, "because now he's in the side yard, and this is no joke."

Ted gave his brother a sharp look. "Now see here. You've bothered me enough. Once is funny, but —" he stopped because he had seen a large spotted animal in the flower bed outside the window.

"You do see it, too, don't you, Ted?"

Ted rushed to the window. The large spotted animal **was** a giraffe!

Finding the Owner

"I hope that this will be a lesson to you," said Jim. "Next time maybe you'll believe me."

"Stop talking," Ted cried. "What are we going to do about this — this beast?"

Jim looked out at the giraffe, which had left the flower bed and was now eating the leaves from an oak tree. The giraffe's head was out of sight, and its long thin neck looked like a large spotted snake. "I read a library book once for a lesson," said Jim.

"This is no time to talk about a book," his brother told him. "Great guns! We've got to **do** something."

"This book," said Jim, "said that giraffes can run faster than most horses."

"What! We've got to catch him. He probably belongs to the zoo."

"Maybe it would be better just to leave him alone," said Jim. "The book I read also said that giraffes kick with their hind legs."

Ted, who had been about to leave the house, stopped. "Perhaps we had better call the zoo first."

"You watch the giraffe, and I'll call the zoo." Jim reached for the telephone book. "Redwood 2-0123. Please hurry . . . Hello, hello. Look, this is Jim Butterfield, out on Diamond Road. We've got a giraffe here in our side yard . . . **a giraffe.** One of those tall, thin animals with long necks from Africa . . ."

Jim stopped suddenly. "What number is this . . . Oh. Oh, I see. I'm sorry." He hung up. "That was the bank."

"Call again," Ted said. "He's eating a bush now."

"Redwood 2–0123," Jim said again into the telephone. "Hello. Is this the zoo? . . . Well, have you lost a giraffe? Yes. Yes? You have? . . . Well, it's here in our flower bed."

"It's in our bushes!" said Ted.

"Bushes," said Jim over the telephone. "What do you want us to do? . . . Thank you. Yes, we will," he said and hung up.

"What did they say?"

"It belongs to the zoo all right. They're sending men out with a truck, and we're to keep the giraffe here until they come." He stopped a moment. "Ted, there's a twenty-five dollar reward for the giraffe. He said we would get the reward, if we caught the giraffe."

"Great!" Ted shouted. "We can buy that camera."

"Projector," said Jim.

"Camera," said Ted.

Ted asked, "Did you say that a giraffe can run faster than a horse? Suppose it runs away when it sees us? Suppose it is frightened by people?"

"Well," said Jim, "I'm afraid of it."

Ted waved his hand. "Don't be silly. Look, you go and get the big animal book and see what it says about giraffes while I watch the beast out of the kitchen window."

Jim rushed off and returned with the book. Ted, who had been watching the giraffe, said, "One of the good things about living in the country is that there's a lot of giraffe food around. He's eating the lily stems now. Mother and Dad won't be pleased."

"If they were home," said Jim, "they could tell Archie about the lily stems."

"Is that his name?"

"That's his name. The zoo man told me." He began to read. "The giraffe lives in Africa, usually in groups of from five to forty. It feeds on leaves and small branches of trees. Yes, we had guessed that."

"If you don't hurry," Ted said, "there won't be any Archie here for us to catch."

Jim read on quickly. "What I said about their kicking with their hind legs is true. But they kick only lions."

"What do you mean, they kick only lions?"

"Well, the lion is their enemy, so, if they meet, the giraffe kicks the lion."

"You and I aren't lions, so Archie won't kick us. Let's go outdoors, Jim."

Jim looked unhappy.

"That twenty-five dollar reward," Ted said, "means we can get that camera."

"Projector," said Jim.

Catching the Giraffe

The boys let themselves carefully out the back door and got within thirty or forty feet of the giraffe before it noticed them. At that point, however, Jim fell over the garden hose and into an empty pail. The noise was so loud that Archie took his head out of the top of the oak tree.

"Sh!" said Ted.

The giraffe looked at the boys. "The man said to be very careful with him," Jim said. "He cost thirty-five hundred dollars."

"He did!" Ted looked at Archie with great interest. "This is going to be quite easy. He's very friendly." He stretched out one hand and began to walk forward, a step at a time. "Here, Archie, Archie. Nice Archie . . ."

Archie gave him one look, turned, and ran around the corner of the house.

"Now see what you've done," said Jim.

"Come on. We've got to catch him," said Ted.

They rushed around the corner of the house and stopped suddenly. The giraffe had found a yellow flower and had decided to have some dessert.

"I have an idea," said Ted. "Let's get him into our barn. It has a high roof, and —"

"May I ask just one question?" said Jim. "How are you going to get him into the barn? You can't lead him, you know. He's all neck and legs. There's nothing to hang onto."

"It will be very easy," Ted told him. "I'll go in front and hold out some grass for him, and you go behind and hang onto his tail."

"Me?" Jim cried. "Hang onto his tail?"

"Certainly. Come on, Jim." Ted gave him a push from behind. Jim looked at Archie's tail for a moment, took a deep breath, and caught hold of it.

After that things happened very quickly. Archie's left leg kicked out and landed a hard blow. Jim rolled over twice on the grass, got to his feet, and started running.

Ted ran after him.

Archie followed the two boys.

Jim and Ted climbed into the branches of the nearest apple tree, and Archie came to a disappointed stop.

The boys looked at each other. "So giraffes kick only lions," said Jim, rubbing his leg.

"You read it in the book yourself," Ted said. He looked thoughtfully down among the branches at Archie's head. The tree was not tall, and Archie was. After a moment Ted broke off some juicy-looking leaves and handed them to Archie. Archie ate them. Ted broke off some more.

Jim got the idea and began to help. "If we can only keep him here until the zoo men come —"

"I hope the tree lasts," said Ted.

Just then a large truck turned into the driveway. "The zoo men!" Ted shouted. "Jim, we're saved." He stopped and added, "But I wish we weren't up here. It doesn't look so good. They might almost think Archie caught us."

The Zoo Keepers Arrive

"Hello!" said a voice. A stout man in blue overalls was looking up at them. He had one arm around Archie's neck. "What are you doing up there?"

Jim said, "We've caught your giraffe for you."

The stout man laughed, and said, "Look who has caught who, will you?"

Ted spoke coolly, "We couldn't find much for him to eat, and we thought feeding him was the best way to keep him here. We're up in this tree getting some more leaves."

Jim and Ted crawled down out of the tree. "Well," the man said finally, "that was pretty smart. Thank you very much. I'll see that you get the reward."

The boys went inside the house. "Now we can get our camera," Ted said.

"**Projector!**" Jim shouted.

"Hmmm," said Ted, "I'll tell you what. Next time we'll buy a projector. This time we'll buy a camera. Now run along and get us some peanut butter cookies. All that work has made me hungry."

Jim looked at his brother, then left the room suddenly. He came back a moment later, with both hands full of cookies and a strange look in his eyes.

"Ted," he said, "I don't like to say so, but there's an elephant in the back yard."

Ted let out a wild scream and rushed into the kitchen. In a minute Jim heard the back door close. A gentle smile came over his face.

Jim looked at the calendar, which still showed that it was April Fool's Day. He smiled again and began to eat his cookies. He felt much better.

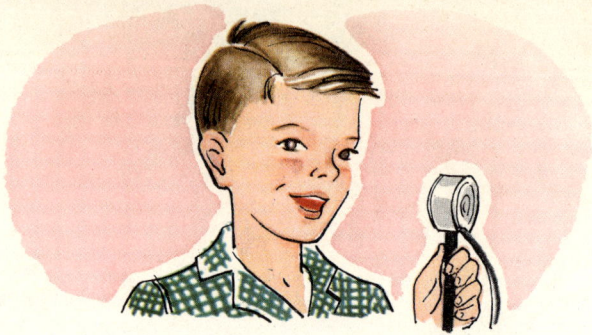

The Country Bunny and the Little Gold Shoes

The Country Bunny

Announcer. Because we hear of the Easter bunny who comes each Easter day before sunrise to bring eggs for boys and girls, we think there is only one bunny. But that is not true. There are really five Easter bunnies. When one of them grows old and can no longer run fast, the kind grandfather bunny who lives at the Palace of Easter Eggs calls forty bunnies together from the whole world. He chooses the very best one to take his place. We now hear a little country girl bunny —

Country Girl Bunny. Some day I shall grow up to be an Easter bunny — you wait and see! You needn't laugh at me and tell me to go back to the country. You just wait and see!

Announcer. The little girl rabbit grew up to be a young lady rabbit. And by and by she had a husband. Then one day, much to her surprise, there were twenty-one fat little baby rabbits to take care of.

Country Mother Bunny. Now, children, since I have such a lovely big family, I'll have to stop thinking about being an Easter bunny who hops all over the world with beautiful eggs for little boys and girls. I'll have to stay at home to take care of my babies.

But because you're such bright little bunnies, we are going to have some fun. I'll teach you two bunnies to sweep the house. You two I'll teach how to make the beds. You two go to the kitchen and learn how to cook a good dinner.

And we'll need two little dishwashers to make the glasses shine. Two more of you can wash all the clothes.

Two can do the sewing and the mending. You two have such sweet voices that you will be taught to sing. Two more can sing and dance for the other bunnies while they work, so all of my children will be gay and happy.

108

Oh! Since the garden must be looked after, you two may plant lettuce and bean seeds in the garden. Now you two take these paints and coloring pencils, and you can make pretty pictures for the walls.

Why, dear me, there is one of my bunnies left who looks sad and lonely. You are the most polite of my children, so I shall make you keeper of my chair. Whenever I come to dinner, you shall seat me politely at the table.

A New Easter Bunny Is Chosen

Announcer. Then one day when the little rabbits were half grown, we hear the mother bunny talking to her children —

Country Mother Bunny. I've just heard that one of the five Easter bunnies is now too slow to deliver the eggs before sunrise on Easter. We will go to the Palace of Easter Eggs to watch Grandfather choose a new one to take his place. How I wish I could be chosen! But that can't happen because I'm an old mother bunny.

Sound. Footsteps of bunnies going to the palace.

Country Mother Bunny. Oh, see! There's kind, wise Grandfather Bunny. Let's stay here and watch.

Grandfather. Now, all you bunnies will take turns running and jumping. Get ready — Go!

Sound. Running of bunnies.

Grandfather. Yes, you are pretty and you are fast, but you have not shown me that you are either kind or wise. Why, look at little Mother Rabbit with all her children. What a large family you have, my dear! I suppose it takes all of your time to care for them.

Country Mother Bunny. They did when they were babies, but they do most of the work for me now.

Grandfather. Ah, you must be very wise. But tell me, do they always look so happy and hold their ears up so prettily?

Country Mother Bunny. Indeed they do! We never have a tear or a cross word in our little country home. And if I do say it myself, they do carry their ears better than most bunnies.

Grandfather. Then you must be very kind indeed to have such a happy home. It is too bad that you have had no time to run and grow swift. I might then have made you my fifth Easter bunny.

Country Mother Bunny (whispers). Let's show Grandfather how fast we can run.

Sound. Running of bunnies.

Grandfather. I see that you are swift, also. It's too bad that you can't carry my eggs. I suppose you'll have to stay home with your children.

Country Mother Bunny. They can take better care of the house than I. These two are my sweepers. These make the beds. These cook my dinner. These wash the dishes. These grow beans and lettuce in the garden. These wash and dry all the clothes. These do the mending. These sing, and the other two dance to keep us merry while we work. These are learning to paint pretty pictures for our walls. And this smallest one politely pulls out my chair for me when I sit at the table. So you see I can leave them.

Grandfather. You are not only wise and kind and swift but also very clever. Come to the palace tomorrow, and you shall be my fifth Easter bunny.

Filling the Baskets

Announcer. The very next evening Mother Bunny knocked on the big front door of the palace. She went into the front room with the other Easter bunnies. There she stood in her funny country bonnet and clothes, but none of the other bunnies laughed. They were wise and kind and knew better. The bunnies showed her all over the palace. They went from room to room piled high with eggs of silver and gold and chocolate. There were eggs for rich children and for poor children, for children who were sick and children who were well, for children all over the world.

Grandfather. Now it's time to fill your baskets with Easter eggs and be on your way to deliver them before sunrise.

Grandfather (after some time). Little Mother Bunny, I know you are tired. You have been filling those baskets for over an hour, but I want you to see this egg. Look through it, and tell me what you see.

Country Mother Bunny. Why, I see a beautiful place with a sleigh and a lake with people skating on the ice. There are children sliding on their sleds, too. Oh! How pretty it is!

Grandfather. You have such a loving heart for children, and you are so clever. I am going to give you, the fifth Easter bunny, the best but the hardest trip of all. Far off, over two rivers and three mountains, there is a great mountain. In a little house by the lake shore on that mountain is a little boy who has been ill for a whole year. He has been so brave that never once has he cried. The mountain is so high that there is ice on the top. It will be hard to climb. If you get there, you will give more happiness than any other Easter bunny. Just take the boy this beautiful Easter egg which shines like a diamond.

The Gold Shoes

Announcer. Mother Bunny put on her bonnet, picked up the egg very gently, and went hopping away on her journey. She climbed over the first mountain and then another and yet another until at last she reached the highest of all. She was very tired when she reached the ice and snow. Now she was almost to the top. She could see the little house all covered with snow by the lake shore. Then a terrible thing happened. Her foot slipped. She rolled across a field and finally struck against an apple tree. There she lay.

Country Mother Bunny. Oh! My leg hurts. I wonder if I can go on. Soon it will be daylight, and the little boy will be sad if he doesn't have an Easter egg. Why, I thought someone touched my shoulder. Oh, hello, Grandfather.

Grandfather. I surprised you didn't I, Mother Bunny? You are not only wise and kind and swift, you are the bravest of all the bunnies. I shall make you my very own gold shoe Easter bunny. Let me put these gold shoes on your feet.

Country Mother Bunny. Why, my leg doesn't hurt any more! I'm sure I can climb the mountain now.

Announcer. Then, before she knew what was happening, she felt herself flying high in the air. Finally she landed right at the door of the little boy's home. Quickly she went through an opening and placed the egg in the hand of the beautiful sleeping boy. And just as the Easter morning sun arose, she hopped quickly back to the palace. There she found a little basket of eggs for her own family.

Country Mother Bunny. I must hurry home now with the pretty Easter eggs for my little bunnies, for they, too, must have a happy Easter.

Sound. Opening of door. Footsteps of Mother Bunny.

Country Mother Bunny. Sure enough! Everything is in fine order. They have done a good job of sweeping. There are two lovely new pictures painted and hung in frames on the wall. The dishes are clean and shining. The clothes are washed and dried, mended and neatly hung up. Yet my twenty-one children are all sound asleep in their beds. Oh! What a happy Easter we are going to have!

Announcer. And now you can always tell little Mother Bunny's house from all the others because of the tiny gold shoes hanging on the wall.

Just for Fun

Jonathan Bing

Poor old Jonathan Bing
Went out in his carriage to visit the
King,
But everyone pointed and said, "Look at
that!
Jonathan Bing has forgotten his hat!"
(He'd forgotten his hat!)

Poor old Jonathan Bing
Went home and put on a new hat for the
King,
But by the palace a soldier said, "Hi!
You can't see the King; you've forgotten
your tie!"
(He'd forgotten his tie!)

Poor old Jonathan Bing,

He put on a beautiful tie for the King,

But when he arrived, an Archbishop said, "Ho!

You can't come to court in pajamas, you know!"

(He'd come in pajamas!)

Poor old Jonathan Bing

Went home and addressed a short note to the King:

"If you please will excuse me, I won't come to tea;

For home's the best place for all people like me!"

Beatrice Curtis Brown

Miss Crumpet's Great Day

Miss Crumpet Meets a Stranger

The people of London were getting ready to crown their new King. Preparations for the great day had gone on for several weeks. Streets were gaily decorated with colored streamers. And in the middle of the preparations stood the tiny candy shop of Miss Crumpet.

Miss Crumpet was a lively little lady, plump, quite short, and always friendly and cheerful. As the Great Day came nearer, Miss Crumpet seemed to lose some of her usual cheerfulness. At first she had watched the preparations in the city square with happiness. As the days passed, she noticed that London grew more and more crowded.

She suddenly realized that she would not be very happy among the large crowds. Her shortness kept her from seeing over other people's heads. She was quite sad because she did want to see **everything**. And then — Professor Beep came to the city!

Did you ever hear of Professor Beep, the great inventor, explorer, and sometimes strong man in the circus? Why, he could invent anything. Once when the King of a far country wanted to know who was coming around the corner before he got there, Professor Beep invented the Around-the-Corner-Looker. The King was so pleased that he gave the Professor a huge reward — an enormous elephant.

One day shortly after the explorer and inventor had arrived in London, he wandered into Miss Crumpet's candy shop near the square.

"And my dear madam," said the Professor to Miss Crumpet, "I suppose that on Coronation Day your shop will be closed, while you watch the great parade?"

"To be sure!" said Miss Crumpet. "I shall close my shop. But how am I to see over the heads of the crowds that will be on the streets to look at the parade?"

"It is true she is rather short, and she is plump, as well," thought Professor Beep. "However, something will have to be done. She seems to be a sweet lady who should have my help." He bowed low.

"My dear madam," said Professor Beep, "I am a great inventor. I must use my head and invent something to help you see the Coronation Parade."

"Ah! If you only could," sighed Miss Crumpet. "But, kind sir, I fear I could not pay for the services of one so great. You must charge for such services."

It pleased the Professor to have Miss Crumpet recognize his greatness so quickly, and he explained that there would be no charge for his services. With that he cried, "Good day, fair lady, I am off to serve you."

The Bouncing Boots

But day followed day. Professor Beep could think of nothing to help Miss Crumpet.

"Even if she could be stretched, she could not be stretched enough," thought the professor. The day of the Coronation drew nearer.

While the Professor was walking through the zoo the next morning, he saw a kangaroo give a mighty jump. As soon as he saw that kangaroo jump, he rushed home. He hurried to his trunk and brought out a pair of boots. Holding the boots closely, he started for Miss Crumpet's shop.

When Professor Beep arrived at her shop, he found her sitting on her doorstep weeping. "And why are you weeping, my little Pet?" he said. The Professor felt he had known Miss Crumpet long enough to shorten her name. For some reason he called her "my little Pet" rather than "my little Crum."

"I weep because I shall not see the parade," said she. "Tomorrow is the Great Day, and you have failed me."

"Not so, my little Crum, I mean Pet," cried the Professor. With a wave of his hand, he brought the boots from behind his back. "Behold!"

"Worrying about me has driven the poor man out of his head," thought Miss Crumpet. "What use can boots be?"

But the Professor was busy. The children stood about with wide-open eyes listening and watching as he drew on the boots. Then he jumped lightly and bounded into the air like a kangaroo.

"Come back," cried the children. Before the words were out of their mouths, the Professor had disappeared around the corner. The children ran after him, but they had scarcely gone ten steps when they heard a voice saying, "Where to, my little friends?"

They turned around, and there was Professor Beep! He had bounded around the block as quick as a wink.

131

"But how will the Bouncing Boots help Miss Crumpet?" asked the children.

"Goodness, I never thought of that," said the Professor. "I must invent something at once, for the Coronation is tomorrow."

As the Professor bounded away, Miss Crumpet thought, "He is a dear man, but he seems a bit silly at times. I know I shall never see the parade." And she started weeping again.

Professor Beep bounded away toward his home. He well remembered the day when the boots had been invented. He had been exploring in South America. No, he must have been in South Africa. He couldn't remember where it was.

Anyway, they were after him, tooth and nail. He had to escape them. They were coming closer, and then he came to an empty blockhouse. Or was it a castle? He couldn't remember. All he could remember was that he had to escape.

He hurried into the — whatever it was — and at once saw a pot of some strange-smelling mixture bubbling over a fire. The pot overturned, and the strange bubbling mixture poured out onto the floor. He stepped into the mixture and out of it. The mixture hardened on his boots, and he found himself bouncing a bit each time he stepped. He stepped into the mixture and out again to let it harden.

He did this many times. Each time a layer was added to the bottom of his boots, he found that he bounded higher into the air. One time he stepped down too hard, and his head went right through the dried grass roof of the blockhouse. Or was it the castle? He couldn't remember. Anyway, he escaped.

By this time his enemies had almost reached him. He heard their angry yells through the forest. He carefully left wherever he was, and once in the open air he gave a mighty jump. Up he flew over the tree tops, but he came straight down again in the same spot. He tried again, but this time he bounded forward.

He came back years later to measure the distance he had bounded forward and found it measured something less than five hundred feet . . . but it had been far enough. He had bounded all that day until he reached a village. By that time he was tired of the boots and never wore them again until today.

When the Professor reached his home, he thought for a few hours. Then he went to the market place and bought a number of things. One of the things he bought was a rocking chair. That evening he was very happy as he went to bed. He knew he would not fail Miss Crumpet.

Miss Crumpet Sees the Coronation

The day of the Coronation arrived. Miss Crumpet sat on her doorstep for a long time. She had given up all hope of seeing the Parade. Suddenly a strange sight met her eyes. It seemed impossible! Yes, it was — it was Professor Beep. What in the world was on his shoulders? It looked like a rocking chair. So it was! When the Professor arrived at her doorstep, he reached down and lifted Miss Crumpet and her umbrella high into the chair. Miss Crumpet screamed with fright, but Professor Beep soon quieted her.

"And now, please tighten across your lap that strap on the side of the chair," said the Professor. "We're going traveling."

Miss Crumpet did as she was told and tightened the strap. The Professor called, "Here we go," and gave a gentle bound into the air. Up they flew, and Miss Crumpet was so surprised that she forgot to be frightened. Professor Beep bounced away so gently that it was almost like sitting home in one's rocking chair.

"I can see everything for blocks and blocks," cried Miss Crumpet. And that, of course, was the Professor's plan.

Now Miss Crumpet could see over the
heads of everybody. People turned to stare
as the Professor bounded along. The people
realized how easily both Miss Crumpet and
the Professor saw everything without
stretching their necks.

Miss Crumpet was too busy watching the
parade to see the people at all. She looked
at the bright colors, the beautiful clothing,
and the gaily decorated horses and coaches
until she became tired. Suddenly she
looked down at the crowds and discovered
something was missing. She had nothing
to wave — but her umbrella. She didn't
even have a camera.

"Professor Beep," she called, "you must let me down a moment."

As the Professor lifted her to the ground, she said, "Professor, I must have a banner to wave. I need a camera to take some pictures, too."

He felt better immediately. Why, she was enjoying herself so much she felt she must wave a banner, and shout, and tell the world about it. Very well, she should have banners and balloons. But it suddenly came to him that he had no money.

"Gladly would I buy these things," he said to Miss Crumpet as he bowed to her, "but I have no money."

"No money?" said Miss Crumpet.

"No money," said the Professor.

They looked at each other sadly.

"That is too bad," said Miss Crumpet.

"Yes," said the Professor. "But let me think for a moment. Perhaps an idea will come to me."

Miss Crumpet fixed her clothing and sat
down while the Professor thought.
Suddenly the Professor jumped up and
looked as if he were going to shake Miss
Crumpet — just a happy cheerful shake.
But he didn't. Instead he said, "The
answer is easy. These people have been
watching us and wishing they could see
the parade as well. Many of them in the
back rows can scarcely see a thing. I shall
rent the chair so they can see the sights,
and for this small service they shall pay
me." With these words the Professor
bounded away to the back rows.

140

Many people wanted to rent the chair, and soon he had enough money to buy some banners, flags, and balloons for Miss Crumpet. And last of all he bought a small camera.

Miss Crumpet was lifted to her chair. How happily she waved her banners and flags! How gaily she let loose her balloons! She cheered the King and Queen. Carefully Miss Crumpet snapped their pictures in their beautiful robes with her camera.

The parade was over, and Miss Crumpet was tired. But she was not too tired to give one final cheer and wave her flags for Professor Beep who had made this wonderful day come true.

Finally the Professor stopped bouncing. He looked up at Miss Crumpet and discovered that she was fast asleep. She was all tired out, but she had a most happy smile on her face. The Professor brought her to her own door. There he awakened her, loosened the strap, and gently let her down. Then he said, "Miss Crumpet, has it been a happy day?"

"Oh, Professor!" said Miss Crumpet. "The most wonderful day of my life. If only — if only the King had sat still and bobbed up and down less."

If I Were an Elephant

If I had an elephant's floppy ears,
I'd wash them once in seven years,
I'd use my trunk for a garden hose
And make a nozzle out of my nose.

Merle Crowell

143

Daniel's Elephant

The Summer Boarder

Nobody was much surprised when Henry Web, who had stopped at the crossroad store for some bread, returned home with a full-grown elephant.

Henry was well known as a friend of animals. People called him the most kindhearted man in town.

He gave up raising geese because he did not like to send them to market. He felt the same way about calves, and he could not even make himself eat an old hen for Sunday dinner.

The day Henry Web went to the store for the bread, he found two strangers talking to Bill Rose, the storekeeper. Bill was shaking his head when Henry came into the store.

"Don't know of anybody who wants that kind of summer boarder," Bill was saying.

Then he saw Henry. "Just a second!" said Bill. "Yes, I do. And here he is now. Gentlemen, this is Mr. Web."

One of the strangers was the owner of Jackson's Circus and Zoo. The other man had been a clown and now looked after the elephants in the circus.

Mr. Jackson explained his business. The circus was a small show. It had three elephants. The name of one of the elephants was Wanda. She had been sick but was just beginning to feel better.

145

"The doctor from the city zoo ordered a rest and a change for Wanda. Now we're looking for a place to board her for a few months. She needs a quiet place where the people like animals. Do you have any children, Mr. Web?"

"Five," said Henry. "Three of them are boys."

"You're in luck! Your children can have Wanda for a playmate for the summer months and at no cost to you. What's more, I'll pay you for her board!"

It was the part about his children having a playmate that made Henry decide to take Wanda home.

How often he had wished that the children and Mrs. Web might have a little fun! But life on a farm — a poor man's farm — isn't much fun for anybody. They had no car or radio. Why a real, live elephant was just the thing! Better than any toy! They could all ride on her back. So Henry went to meet Wanda with some peanuts in his hand.

She was a huge elephant, and she looked very dusty at first sight. Henry was not sure she would fit into his barn.

He was about to say she wouldn't fit into his barn when his pale blue eyes met Wanda's eyes. They were old and wise eyes that had looked at many, many people. Her eyes now looked at Henry with a question.

A friendly feeling of understanding passed between Henry and Wanda.

"Well," said Henry, "I don't know what my wife will say — but I'll try it."

Mrs. Web Puts Her Foot Down

Henry rode back to the farm seated on Wanda's head right up behind her ear. The elephant man taught him what to say to Wanda to make her put her trunk around him and lift him up there. He told Henry a lot of elephant words which Henry wrote on the pages of a notebook.

Mrs. Web, meanwhile, was busy in the kitchen salting some squash. She was a thin, sharp-tongued little woman. Sometimes she thought Henry was too kindhearted to all stray animals.

The five Web children were helping their mother. The oldest were Ada and Albert, who were twins. Next came Beulah, ten years old. Then came Canfield, who was eight, and last of all Daniel, who was just six.

All the Web children had pale blue eyes just like their father. All of the children liked animals, too.

Mrs. Web was saying, "Your father is late, and supper is ready. Probably he has heard of a stray dog or cat. He's too kindhearted for his own good. With a man like your father there is no telling. Nothing he can do — nothing — would surprise me . . ."

Mrs. Web, who had been looking out the kitchen window, ended with a scream. She turned pale and moved her hands quickly as if to push away what she saw.

"No!" she cried. "Henry Web, this is the end!"

The five Web children joined their mother in looking out the window.

"Oh!" cried Albert.

"Oh!" cried Ada, his twin sister.

Beulah said, "Why it's . . . it's . . ."

"An elephant," said Canfield, and Daniel spoke up, "An elephant, an elephant!"

Daniel led them all as they rushed from the house to meet Henry and Wanda. The others stopped before the huge animal, but Daniel rushed up to her and threw his arms about her. That is, since he was very small even for six, he threw his arms about her leg in his most friendly way.

The tip of Wanda's trunk felt over the small boy whose arms were around her leg. Wanda liked Daniel immediately.

There were danger signals in Mrs. Web's snapping black eyes. "I might have known it," she cried. "My mother told me this would happen some day. Now . . . you've done it!"

Seated on Wanda's head, high above them, Mr. Web realized that his wife was angry. He tried to make a joke. "I brought you a little present from town, Lucy."

"Henry Web, you come down here."

"Yes, dear," Henry said softly.

151

He turned the pages of his notebook, looking for the elephant words. When he spoke them, Wanda reached up with her strong trunk and lifted him to the ground gently.

"See," said Henry. "She is as gentle as a kitten and very intelligent. You'll love her, Lucy."

He began to talk very fast, telling his wife just how he happened to hear about Wanda, and what a good chance this was to give the children a playmate and to help Mr. Jackson be kind to a poor, sick animal and to be paid for it in the bargain.

Mrs. Web said, "Henry, either that elephant leaves here, or I do."

152

Mrs. Web walked back to the kitchen. Henry and the children watched in silence. Daniel was the first to speak.

"Can't we keep our elephant, Papa? Can't we?"

"Son," said Henry sadly, "your mother is a wonderful woman. But when she puts her foot down . . . well, she puts it down very hard. I guess Wanda will have to go back."

After supper the children went to bed. But as soon as they thought their parents were asleep, they gathered for a talk. Wanda must stay on the farm. But how?

Daniel Gets an Idea

Albert, as the oldest, led the meeting. "All those who want to keep Wanda raise their hands," he said in a very businesslike way. They all raised their hands.

"The chair will now listen to any suggestions," said Albert. "Does anybody have any ideas?"

There was a great silence.

Finally Beulah said, "If we wrote a letter to mother asking her, she might let us keep Wanda."

"We have asked her, and she said no," said Daniel.

"We could have a strike like those men who are working for Mr. Brown," said Canfield.

"It would only make Mama angrier," sighed Ada.

"And we would get a spanking," added Daniel.

They all agreed that a strike only meant a spanking.

"All right," said Albert. "Ada, do you have an intelligent suggestion?"

Ada said that she hadn't.

"Maybe Mama will change her mind by morning," Beulah said.

Daniel spoke up. "I have an idea."

"What is it?" they asked.

But Daniel wouldn't tell. "I'll have to think about it," he said.

They all laughed and said, "That's fine. Think about it, Daniel. You're smart."

But they didn't really believe him. After all, he was only six.

"I guess the meeting is over," said Albert
sadly. So they all went to bed.

Daniel lay awake, thinking of Wanda
and his plan. He was a very thoughtful
little boy. When he wanted something he
could think of nothing else. And Daniel
wanted Wanda to stay on the farm!

After a long time he slipped out of bed.
He put on his bathrobe and slippers by the
light of the moon and went out to the barn.

Wanda, whose back leg was chained to
a log, was nervous in her new home with
the mice. She rocked back and forth.

156

When Daniel spoke her name, Wanda raised her trunk. Slowly, like a mountain moving, she knelt before the little boy. Her chain rattled in the dark.

Daniel came closer. He whispered in her enormous ear, "Don't feel bad, Wanda. We like you. I won't let Mama send you away."

Wanda might not have understood what the words meant, but she knew they were friendly. She forgot to be homesick and nervous about the mice. The pair of them slept close together in their bed of clean hay.

Daniel's Idea

The small boy awakened with the first sign of light. He hurried back to the house and got into bed. He knew his mother would spank him if she knew he had been sleeping in the hay in the barn all that night.

After breakfast Mr. Web appeared, leading Wanda. The family gathered to tell the elephant good-by.

"I may be back in time for the milking," Henry sighed very nervously. "Jackson's Circus has moved over to the next town. Wanda can't travel five miles very fast."

"Never mind that," said his wife. "You just see that she travels out of my sight forever."

"Oh, Mama!" Albert cried. "We were going to have such fun with her."

"We were going to take rides on her," added Ada.

"Please, Mama!" Canfield begged, and tears came to Beulah's eyes.

Mrs. Web stood in silence, but one look at the danger signals in her eyes told them how she felt.

His brothers and sisters turned to Daniel. "You ask her," they begged. "Maybe she'll listen to you. You said you had an idea."

"Maybe my idea is no good," Daniel answered. "I — I'll try if Papa will help me." He and his father walked away from the family and talked together. Mr. Web looked uncertain. Then he smiled and nodded. Then he looked uncertain again.

"Your mother has made up her mind. But you never know," he said.

"I have just thought of something," Henry said to his wife. "Do you remember that big old millstone that we used for a step up to the back porch? The truck carried it out to the field when the carpenters fixed the porch. We could never afford to have it put back again. Let's have Wanda move the millstone before she goes."

Mrs. Web said, "That great lazy lump can't move a millstone!"

"She is not lazy," said Daniel. "Wanda is a good elephant. Come on, Wanda."

The old millstone had been lying in the tall weeds ever since the carpenters had fixed the back porch. The Web family and Wanda gathered around the millstone in the tall weeds.

Henry looked in his notebook with the elephant words in it. He turned the pages back and forth.

"It doesn't say anything about lifting rocks with her tusks," he exclaimed. "There aren't any words for it."

"O-o-oh! Look again, Papa."

"It's no use," said their father.

"Told you so!" said Mrs. Web. "All that lazy elephant is good for is to eat us out of house and home! We can't afford to keep her."

"Papa, let me try," Daniel cried.

"You!" they exclaimed.

"She'll do it for me because we're friends," Daniel said. "Please, let me try to do it!"

He waved his family away and stood alone before the enormous elephant. "Down, Wanda," he ordered, and Wanda sank slowly to her knees in the tall weeds. Daniel scrambled up on her shoulder and whispered into her huge ear, "Please, Wanda, be a good elephant and watch what I do!"

Then he scrambled down again, went over to the old millstone, knelt down, and pretended to lift it up.

"See, Wanda? Up? Lift it?"

Wanda's intelligent little eyes followed every move he made. Her great head began to nod rapidly. She sank down beside Daniel, feeling over the stone with the tip of her trunk and slipping her big tusks under it. Slowly she began to lift the stone from the ground.

"Good elephant!" cried Daniel.

"Up! Up, Wanda!" cried Mrs. Web. The family cheered.

Wanda had lifted the stone with her trunk. She held it on her tusks. She moved carefully to her feet and waited. Led by Daniel, they went slowly to the kitchen porch where Wanda set the stone in the spot as gently as if it were a box of fresh eggs.

"Henry," said Mrs. Web, "I thought you told me that Wanda was sick."

"She's getting better now, Lucy. The doctor says a little work is good for her."

Mrs. Web looked thoughtful. "Do you think she could move that big old tree that is too near the house?"

Henry looked at his youngest son.

Daniel nodded his head rapidly.

"Of course she can, Lucy. Daniel, you may tell her what to do."

Now that Wanda had the idea, she moved the old tree in a short time.

Mrs. Web was very happy. For years she had wished that the old tree could be taken away and that the millstone was back where it could be used as a step. But she was not going to say she had been wrong. She looked up to see a few clouds in the sky.

"Look at that sky," she said. "Anybody can see that a lightning storm is coming. You had better not take that poor, sick animal back to the circus today. Why don't you take her back tomorrow or even next week? If a little work is what the doctor ordered, there are some things she can do right around here. What are you smiling at?" she asked sharply.

"I wasn't smiling, Lucy," Henry said gently. "I was just thinking that you had hit upon a very good idea! Let's keep Wanda for a few days."

"We'll see," said his wife.

The Web family cheered.

Anybody who knew Mrs. Web knew that her "we'll see" meant that Wanda could stay on the farm as long as she wished.

Everybody for miles around heard of Henry Web and Wanda. Again they said that he certainly was the most kindhearted man in the state. But when they went to the farm to see Wanda for themselves — and they all did — they changed their minds.

Wanda had moved so many stones from Henry's field that he began to raise all the vegetable crops the family needed and some more which he sold. And when Wanda wasn't working for Henry, he rented her to his neighbors who wished stones and trees moved.

The work did Wanda good. Henry Web was able to save enough money from renting her to put in the bank.

"That Henry Web is the smartest man in the state," said his neighbors.

But Henry said, "Not nearly so smart as my little boy, Daniel. It was all his idea."

Kippie the Cow

A Cow Who Knows Her Own Mind

Far, far away across a large ocean lies a little country. There, in the middle of farmland but not very far south of a big city by the sea, was a beautiful old farmhouse. It was the home of Kristen Manson, his wife, and their four children.

The Mansons had a horse, a pig, and a goat, but most important of all were the cows and calves. The only thing which they did not have sometimes was money. But, as you well know, that is not very important.

They liked their cows and calves and were very proud of them. Kippie the Cow was the largest of the cattle.

There were many mouths to be fed, and the children needed good warm clothing for school. All of this costs a lot of money. The time came when Kristen Manson, the farmer, could not make ends meet. So he said to his wife, "I think we are going to sell Kippie."

"That's easy to say. But how do you know that she'll want to be sold?" asked Mrs. Manson uncertainly.

"I am master of the farm, and I decide what is to be done," replied Kristen.

The children cried when they heard that
Kippie was to be sold. One morning a
week later in February they got up early
to say good-by to her. "Please don't leave
us, please stay with us, dear Kippie the
Cow," they begged.

But Kippie the Cow was a strong-minded
beast. She had decided that she wanted
to leave the farm and see the world. She
started off slowly down the road.

"There, you see, I shall have no trouble
getting her to the city," said Kristen
Manson. He grabbed his hat and cane and
hurried to catch up with Kippie.

They walked quickly, for Kippie the Cow had made up her mind to see the world and try her luck. The road went up a hill. When they reached the top, they were able to see the big city and the harbor in the distance. It was still so early that people were just beginning to go to work. Everyone looked at Kristen Manson with curiosity.

All this attention rather went to Kristen Manson's head, and he wanted to show off a little. So he gave his cow a light tap with his cane and said, "Get along there, and get a move on you. I want to be at the fair before six o'clock so that I can sell you."

Now this tap was the wrong thing to do. Kippie the Cow turned around and gave Kristen Manson a surprised look. At this he gave her another tap with his cane. Immediately she stopped in the middle of the road.

Kristen Manson didn't like that at all. If he were late for the fair, he would not be able to sell his cow. Besides he didn't want everyone to see how his cow disobeyed. Perhaps he would have to take Kippie the Cow home again. His wife would see that she had been right when she had said, "How do you know that Kippie the Cow wants to be sold?"

"I'd better smoke my pipe and think," he said to himself. He sat down on a stone and lighted his pipe. Kristen tried to think very deeply.

Kippie the Cow looked at him. She had enjoyed disobeying her master. But now she was tired of waiting. She stamped the road, leaped up and down, and looked at Kristen Manson.

"Be quiet there," he said, "and wait until I've finished my pipe."

As soon as Kippie the Cow understood that she was free to stand there, she decided to move on again.

"Wait a moment. I'll come in a little while," Kristen Manson called.

Kippie the Cow knew what she wanted. She disobeyed and walked ahead. When she heard her master running after her, she swished her tail and began to trot down the hill toward the city. Kippie was going to the city now.

Kippie Rides the Trolley Car

Kippie discovered that she enjoyed running, so she ran as fast as she could. Oh! She was very pleased with herself! By now she was so far ahead that Kristen Manson would not be able to catch up with her. Soon she came to the edge of the city where the first trolley car started into the city.

Kippie the Cow went up to the trolley car, gave it a kick, and stamped her feet. A cow is even more curious than a man, and Kippie had never seen a trolley before. After she had kicked it several times, she felt she had to find out what the inside of the car looked like. She put both of her front legs on the step and was just going to hop in at the back door when the conductor saw her.

"Hello there!" he shouted. "Get out! This is no cow trolley!"

Before Kristen could rush over to where the trolley was standing, Kippie the Cow had entered the doorway. The conductor came just in time to put up the chain at the back door to stop Kippie from going any farther into the car. She had to stay right in the doorway of the trolley, which was not very comfortable. Besides, she had no room to turn either to the right or to the left.

"Hang it all! We must get her out of here," said the driver.

"Oh, no! We must start right away," said the conductor. "We're late already." He closed the doors, and the trolley car started to move.

At the next stop several people were waiting for the trolley car. They stared in wide-eyed surprise at Kippie.

"What in the world is that?" asked one of the curious passengers.

"That's a cow," said the conductor. "You'll have to enter by the front door."

"Has the cow paid her money?" asked a smiling gentleman.

"If she's under five years old she goes free," said a young girl.

"Only if you're willing to take her on your lap," the conductor said.

But the girl thought this wouldn't be very comfortable.

The passengers joked and had a good time. By and by the trolley reached the edge of the fair grounds.

"We have to make a short stop here," the conductor told the passengers.

He called loudly for some men to help him. They brought a long board and pushed it under Kippie, so that she could slide out backwards.

When she was down, she stood on the edge of the fair grounds and looked around.

"What shall we do with her?" asked one of the men.

"I would send her to the Lost and Found office," said a boy. "Maybe they have some rule about cows."

Curious people came from all sides to see the cow who had come by trolley car. Soon a large excited crowd gathered. Then a policeman blew his whistle.

"Keep moving," he shouted. "Anybody who blocks traffic will be arrested and taken to the police station."

When he saw the cow, he didn't know what to do. There was nothing in his rule book about arresting a cow.

At that moment another trolley car arrived, and out stepped Kristen Manson. He went up to Kippie the Cow and spoke to her.

"You are a fine one!" he said. "But I must say that you're rather smart. Who would have thought that you would take the trolley car? I'm sorry that I have to part with you."

"Moo!" said Kippie the Cow.

"How much do you want for her?" a man from a newspaper office asked.

"I don't even know that you can afford her," said Kristen Manson. "First of all I would like something to eat, and then we'll see what's what. The cow should have something to eat and drink, too. That is, if she wants something, for she's a cow who knows her own mind."

"Moo," said Kippie in a way which showed that she had nothing against a bite to eat. So she was given water and hay. While she ate, Kristen crossed through the traffic to a small restaurant. He sat down at a table near the window, from which he could watch Kippie while he ate.

Kippie Is Famous

In the meantime, the news of the cow who had taken a trolley car spread throughout the city. More newspaper men arrived to get the story of this unusual animal.

First they tried to talk with Kippie the Cow, but of course she refused to answer all their foolish questions. So they did the next best thing. They found the famous cow's master in the restaurant and talked with Kristen Manson. They took his picture, alone, and with Kippie.

Though he was excited, Kristen Manson was clearheaded enough to see that Kippie was not an ordinary cow who could be sold to anybody. She had become famous. Now the whole country would be talking about her.

But what was he to do? He thought and thought and moved his hat about on his head and scratched himself behind the ear. He was in a very bad spot because he had told people that Kippie the Cow had come here to be sold. Now everybody wanted to buy her. Who wouldn't like to own the famous cow? She had taken a ride to the fair in a trolley car, and her picture was in all the newspapers and even on television.

"I will give you one hundred dollars," said the first man.

Another man pushed forward in the crowd. "I'll give you one hundred thirty dollars for the cow," the man shouted.

180

"I'll give you one hundred thirty-five dollars," said another.

"And I one hundred forty-five dollars . . ." And so it went up to two hundred fifty dollars.

Kristen Manson said not a word. He finished his cup of soup. Then he pounded on the table so loudly that the cups rattled.

"The cow costs one hundred fifty dollars — no more and no less," he said. "That's what I decided when I left home. You can have her for one hundred fifty dollars. The buyer must first show me that he can lead her home though. The charge for trying is fifteen dollars. The money has to be put right here on the table. If the cow doesn't want to be led away, the money becomes mine."

Everyone smiled because each one of the men thought that he could lead the small cow away.

The foolish man who had wished to pay two hundred fifty dollars wanted the first chance. He laid fifteen dollars on the restaurant table in front of Kristen Manson and went out. He went over to Kippie and took hold of her rope, while the crowd waited to see the lucky buyer walk away with the prize cow. The fellow gave the rope a sharp pull. Nothing happened. He pulled and shouted, but Kippie the Cow knew her own mind. The man talked to her until he was out of breath. Yet Kippie held her ground. Finally the buyer became angry and walked off without the prize cow.

Then the next man came forth. He also put fifteen dollars on the restaurant table in front of Kristen. He walked over to a vegetable store and bought the biggest carrot he could find. With this he tried to get Kippie the Cow to follow him. Kippie the Cow looked off into the distance and refused to even see the carrot. At last the disappointed man gave up and walked off.

Now a third man, whose mind was made up that Kippie would go with him, took his turn. The third man was a large fellow with high boots, and in his hand he carried a riding whip. When he saw that Kippie the Cow did not move when her rope was pulled, he kicked her with his boots and struck her with his whip. But it didn't help at all. Kippie looked angrily at him and stamped her feet. Neither did she move even when he struck her again with his whip.

One after another they came up to take a chance for the prize. Kippie the Cow still refused to move.

When the last buyer had failed, Kristen Manson pounded the table again and said, "Enough, enough — you can't work on my poor cow forever. Now I'll show you that the cow will come with me of her own free will without my touching the rope. Then I'll come back and take my money."

Everyone agreed that this was a fair rule. No one believed that Kristen Manson would be able to make this stubborn beast follow him willingly. Kristen went outside to Kippie.

"Listen now, Kippie," he said. "I have to return home tonight, but you can do whatever you please. First I have to go back to the restaurant and pick up my money. Mind you, I don't want you following me."

What a surprise it was for everybody to see Kippie the stubborn Cow come trotting after her master!

Yes, if Kristen hadn't closed the door in her face she would have come right into the restaurant.

Everyone roared with laughter and agreed that Kristen Manson had earned his money. He put the one hundred fifty dollars he had won in his pocket.

Kippie the Cow Goes Home

"Good-by, Kippie," said Kristen Manson when he came out again. "Now I'm on my way home. You can stay here if you like. The place under those stairs would make a nice spot to sleep. Maybe you'd rather go home with one of those men who wanted to buy you. Or maybe the policeman will arrest you and take you to the police station. But I don't want to have you with me, do you understand? Let this be a lesson to you." Without another word he walked away down the street.

When Kippie the Cow understood that Kristen Manson wanted to leave her, she felt a strong wish to go along with him. She trotted along after him. Wanting to go much faster, she put her nose against his back and pushed him forward.

The crowd laughed loudly and cheered Kristen Manson and Kippie the Cow. But Kippie the Cow did not pay any attention to the people. She was hurrying Kristen along so fast that he had all he could do to stay on his feet.

"Try to walk a little faster," said Kristen, having learned his lesson, and immediately Kippie dragged along.

And so it went the whole way home. He had discovered the secret of getting along with a stubborn cow who knew her own mind.

After a long walk they came in sight of their house. The whole family — mother, children, farm animals — were waiting by the road for Kristen to come home.

"What did I tell you?" said his wife. "I know Kippie. She is a cow who knows her own mind."

Silently Kristen Manson reached in his pocket and showed his wife the one hundred fifty dollars. How could he earn the money and keep the cow, too?

"You will read all about it in the newspaper tomorrow," said Kristen Manson.

The children were very happy. They put their arms around Kippie the Cow and patted her sides. Then they tried to lead her into the barn, for they had filled her box with sweet-smelling fresh hay. But Kippie the stubborn Cow refused to move.

189

Mrs. Manson brought a pail of water and tried to lead Kippie into the barn. But before the mother knew what was happening, Kippie was drinking from the pail of water.

"No, you don't know how to get along with Kippie the Cow," her husband said. "The only one who can make her behave is your husband."

He went up to Kippie and whispered into her ear. He said, "Don't go into the barn or eat out of your box of hay. It's for a new calf."

Immediately Kippie the Cow walked into the barn.

"There, you see! I can make her do as I wish," said Kristen Manson. "You must tell her in just the right way."

Then the whole family went happily into the house to eat their supper, while Kippie the Cow ate her sweet-smelling hay and carrots.

Eddie's Adventures

Eddie and Gardenia

Gardenia Trouble

Eddie Wilson had a pet goat named Gardenia. Gardenia was only happy when she was eating something or had climbed up on top of something. The happier Gardenia was, the unhappier Eddie's father and mother were.

One Monday afternoon Gardenia got out of her fenced yard and climbed on top of Mr. Wilson's new car. This would not have been so bad, but Gardenia began to eat the cloth top of the car.

When Mr. Wilson came home from his office, there was Gardenia chewing a mouthful of car. Her face was turned up to the sky, and her eyes were closed in enjoyment. At her feet there was a big hole in the canvas top.

Mr. Wilson was carrying a newspaper under his arm. He rolled it up, threw it at Gardenia, and shouted, "Get down off there, you good-for-nothing goat!"

Gardenia was so surprised that she leaped into the air. When she came down, her two front feet sank right through the hole she had chewed in the canvas top of the car. She sat down on her hind legs on the roof.

This made Mr. Wilson shout louder. The louder he shouted, the harder Gardenia kicked her front legs. They were now hanging down inside the automobile.

Eddie and his three brothers were having a ball game up the street behind the firehouse when they heard their father shouting. Fast as arrows they came racing home from their ball game. When they reached their driveway, they saw Gardenia sitting on top of their father's new car. All the boys began to shout.

When Mr. Wilson saw the boys, he cried, "Edward Wilson! If I ever get that goat down off that automobile, it's going to be the end of her. Rudy, get me a ladder! Frank, get me a rope! John, pick up my hat! Eddie, do something! Get inside the car and hold her legs before she kicks off the whole canvas top!"

Eddie got inside the car. He reached up and grabbed Gardenia's front legs.

194

"Boys!" cried Mr. Wilson. "Hurry up with the ladder."

"Here it is," cried Rudy. "Do you want me to go up and get her?"

"I'll get her," said Mr. Wilson.

"Here's the rope," Frank shouted.

"I don't need any rope. Why did you bring a rope?"

"You told me to get a rope, Dad."

By this time Mr. Wilson had his hands on Gardenia and was pulling at her. He couldn't get her loose. She was stuck tight.

"Papa!" cried Eddie, from inside the automobile. "I can't hold her. She's pulling away."

"Let go! Let go!" shouted Mr. Wilson. "How can I get her loose if you hold on to her legs?"

"You told me to hold on to her legs, Papa," Eddie cried.

"Well, let go of them now!"

Eddie let go, and Gardenia's legs flew up through the hole in the canvas top.

In a few moments Mr. Wilson had the goat by the collar. He climbed down the ladder and set her on the ground. Eddie took hold of her collar and dragged her through the gate and into her corral. He gave her a hard slap and said, "You're more trouble than you're worth. Why can't you stay where you belong? You're always getting me into trouble."

Gardenia just walked away to get a mouthful of hay. Her face was turned up in enjoyment, and her eyes were half shut. She was having a little dessert.

Plans for Gardenia

Eddie stayed outside until his mother called him for dinner. Eddie knew his father was very angry. He knew because Papa had called him Edward.

Eddie washed his hands and dried them on a towel. Then he looked into the mirror. He took his comb and combed his hair without being told. He slipped silently into his chair at the table.

Mother smiled at him.

Eddie felt better, but only until Papa cleared his throat for the third time.

"Edward," said his father. "That goat must go," his father continued.

"I'm sorry, Papa. I'll give Gardenia to the firemen."

"The firemen won't take her."

"Well, what shall I do with her, Papa?" Eddie asked.

"I think the thing to do with Gardenia," said Mother, "is to ship her down to Uncle Ed's ranch. He has a lot of goats, and one more goat would just be one more goat to Uncle Ed."

"She'd be lonesome," said Eddie, "away off there in Texas."

"Ed can give her his station wagon and tractor to eat, and she'll get over being lonesome," said Mr. Wilson.

Eddie knew better than to say anything about Gardenia.

"Eddie," said his mother, "I want you to write a letter to Uncle Ed and ask him if he'll take Gardenia."

"O.K., Mama," Eddie whispered.

Eddie didn't eat quite so much dinner as he usually did. He didn't have any seconds, not even when it came to dessert. There seemed to be a lump in his throat.

As soon as dinner was over, his mother sent him up to his room to write the letter to Uncle Ed. Eddie hung a sign on his door saying, **Man Working.**

Eddie wrote the letter, then got up from his desk, and went to the head of the stairs. He called down, "Say, Mama! When am I going to Texas to Uncle Ed's ranch?"

"When you are old enough to be a cowboy," Mother called back.

Eddie returned to the letter and wrote, "How old do I have to be to be a cowboy?" Then Eddie took it downstairs for his mother to address and to give to the postman.

Uncle Ed's Reply

About a week later Eddie received an answer to his letter. It was waiting for him on the hall table when he came in from school. He always felt very important when he found a letter lying on the table addressed to him. Quickly Eddie opened the letter.

This is what he read:

Dear Eddie,

I shall be happy to have Gardenia, but I can't feed her automobiles. She'll just have to eat like the rest of the goats. Now about being a cowboy — you are never too young to be a cowboy. Your cousin George is eight and is a very good cowboy. We hope that you will come to the ranch and visit us soon.

With love,
Uncle Ed

At dinner Eddie said, "Papa, cousin George is a cowboy. I wish I could go to the ranch and be a cowboy."

"Why, Eddie," said his mother, "that's just what your father and I have been talking about. I received a letter from Uncle Ed today, too. He wants us to send you down to spend several months on the ranch. Uncle Ed and Aunt Mary feel that your cousin George needs a boy to play with. Maybe you can spend one month there."

"Oh, boy!" cried Eddie. "May I go?"

"We think it's a good idea," said his mother.

"Oh, boy!" was all Eddie could say.

In the middle of undressing for bed, Eddie had an idea. He ran to the head of the stairs and called down, "Papa! May I take Gardenia with me?"

"Go to bed, Eddie," his father called back. "We'll talk about it tomorrow."

When Mrs. Wilson went upstairs to kiss Eddie good night, his eyes were shining like two black diamonds. "Mama! Am I going on an airplane to Uncle Ed's or on a train?"

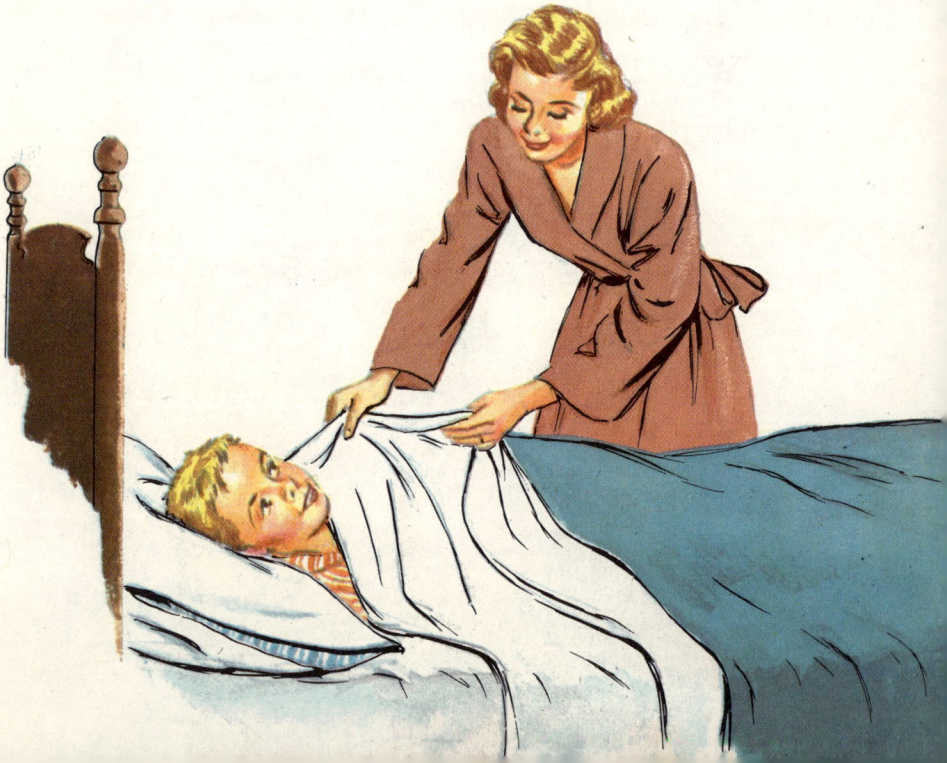

"If you go on the train," said his mother, "you will sleep on the train, and you can take Gardenia in the baggage car. If you fly, you will get there quicker, but Gardenia will have to go by train."

"I'll go on the train," said Eddie. "Will I dress like a cowboy with spurs and ride a horse?"

"Not on the train," said Mrs. Wilson.

Eddie laughed. "I don't mean on the train. Will I wear cowboy clothes and spurs when I get to the ranch?"

"You'll wear whatever George wears," said his mother. "Now go to sleep."

Getting Ready for the Trip

Eddie was to leave in three days. It was more trouble to get Gardenia ready for the trip than Eddie. Mr. Wilson made a box for her and telephoned the railroad office to take her in the baggage car.

Eddie's train was to leave at noon on Monday. He was up at five o'clock that morning, scrambling around like a squirrel. When his father came downstairs, he found Eddie's suitcase by the front door. Mr. Wilson opened the door to pick up the morning paper. He found a box of hay and a large bag of grain on the step.

Mr. Wilson cleared his throat. "What's this?" he asked.

Just then Eddie came leaping through the front hall. "That's for Gardenia to eat on the trip," he said.

"Eddie!" cried his father. "Gardenia couldn't eat that much food in two days! You can take half of the bag of grain," said Mr. Wilson. "That will be more than enough."

Eddie dragged the box of hay past Gardenia's corral back into the barn. He measured the grain carefully. Then he fed Gardenia an enormous breakfast from what was left.

The Trip Begins

When it was time for Eddie and Gardenia to leave for the railroad station, Mr. Wilson drove the old station wagon into the driveway. He put Eddie's suitcase into it. Then he and Rudy carried out the box where they had put Gardenia. Gardenia was making a fearful racket. "Ba-a-a-h! Ba-a-a-h!"

Eddie hopped around in excitement. "It's all right, Gardenia!" he kept saying. "We're going on a trip. You're going to have a good time!"

"Ba-a-a-h! Ba-a-a-h! Ba-a-a-h!" said Gardenia, as the box was lifted into the back of the station wagon.

At the station Mr. Wilson went off to see that Gardenia was put into the baggage car. Mrs. Wilson stood by the gate while Eddie and his brothers stood by the fence. They stared at the streamlined train which would carry Eddie and Gardenia to the state of Texas.

At last the gates were opened. Mr. Wilson returned without Gardenia. All the Wilsons walked through the gates to put Eddie on the streamlined train.

"It's Car Number 124," said Eddie. "Room Number 2."

"Yes, Eddie," said his father, "I know."

In a moment Eddie called out, "Here it is! Number 124."

A porter in a white coat took Eddie's suitcase and showed the Wilsons to Eddie's room.

Mr. Wilson said to the porter, "This is my son Eddie. He's going through to Texas. His aunt and uncle are meeting him. I don't believe he will be any trouble to you."

The porter smiled and said, "Don't worry about your boy, sir. I'll take the same care of him that I'd take of my own boy. I'll deliver him to them."

"Are you sure Gardenia is on the train?" said Eddie. "Gardenia's my goat," he said to the porter. "I'm taking her to Texas."

"She's on the train," said his father.

210

"May I go see her?" asked Eddie. "Where's the baggage car?"

"You can't go up until the train starts," said the porter. "They're busy as bees up there now." He pointed to a button on the wall and said, "When you push that button, I'll come."

"Don't push the button if it's not important, Eddie," said his mother.

Just then they heard the conductor call out, "All aboard!"

Mrs. Wilson kissed Eddie on the forehead and so did his father. His three brothers each gave him a good-by slap on the back.

"Be a good boy," said his mother.

"I will!" promised Eddie.

"And write to us," said his father.

"Sure," said Eddie. And suddenly there were tears in his eyes.

His father and mother and the boys were outside now.

The conductor waved to the engineer. Eddie could hear the engine as the wheels began to turn. Everyone was waving now in excitement. As the streamlined train pulled away, they could hear Gardenia up in the baggage car. "Ba-a-a-h! Ba-a-a-h! Ba-a-a-h!"

Eddie the Cowboy

The Search for Gardenia

Eddie had been on the ranch for several days. Soon after he had come to visit Uncle Ed and Aunt Mary, Eddie and George had taken Gardenia over to the north pasture where the goats were. She had seemed happy to see other goats.

One day after lunch Eddie said, "I guess I'll go over to the pasture and see Gardenia."

"She'll be glad to see you," said Bob, one of the cowboys. "It has been a long time, hasn't it?"

"Sure has," said Eddie. "If I could have an old feed bag, I could tie it to my saddle strap. Then I would have some grain to give Gardenia."

"That's a good idea," said Bob. "I'll get you an old feed bag."

Eddie filled the bag and tied it to his saddle. He climbed up on Sugar, picked up the reins, and they started off for the north pasture.

He looked up at the deep blue sky. He saw an airplane heading toward the airport west of the ranch. As he watched it flying toward the airport, there passed between him and the airplane some big black birds. "Buzzards!" thought Eddie. "They're bad birds. Always waiting to pick the bones of some poor animal that has died."

Finally Eddie arrived at the pasture where he had left Gardenia. He stopped by the fence and looked out over the goats toward the west. He couldn't see Gardenia anywhere.

"It's funny she isn't looking for me," thought Eddie. Then he began to wonder. Maybe she'd forgotten all about him, or maybe she had died.

Eddie got off Sugar and opened the gate. He led him into the pasture and closed the gate. Then he rode slowly all around the pasture. He looked at the goats, his eyes searching for the sight of a collar. "Perhaps," thought Eddie, "her hair has gotten so thick that it hides her collar."

Eddie moved from one group of stray goats to another. The goats paid no attention to Eddie.

He followed the fence all the way around the pasture. Once he looked up. Those buzzards were still there, flapping their great black wings.

Eddie saw many goats that looked like Gardenia, but no goat recognized him. Then the thought came to him that maybe he would never know again which one was Gardenia. Maybe he would look right at her and wouldn't know her. Maybe he was looking at her now. There were so many goats. But it was hard for Eddie to believe that Gardenia wouldn't recognize him.

The Catclaw Bush

At last Eddie reached the far end of the pasture. There were more bushes and trees. Eddie rode all around them.

Just as he was about to give up the search and go home, he noticed a stray goat standing so still that it hardly seemed alive. Its head and most of its body were hidden deep in a bush.

Eddie threw Sugar's reins over the branch of a tree. His heart beat faster. Then he walked all around the bush. It was covered with sharp thorns. Eddie remembered the stories he had heard about the catclaw bush.

Suddenly Eddie realized what the trouble was. The goat was trapped in the bush. Eddie pulled one branch aside. Now he was able to see into the bush. He pulled another branch and scratched his hand. Now he could see the goat's head, and then he saw what he had been looking for all afternoon — a collar under the goat's thick fur.

"Gardenia!" cried Eddie. "Gardenia!"

Gardenia didn't make a sound.

Eddie pulled at the branches, tearing his shirt and scratching himself. There was blood on his fingers and blood on Gardenia's fur. It took a long time to free Gardenia, but finally Eddie cut the claws away from Gardenia's thick fur with a knife. Then when she was free, she sank to the ground at Eddie's feet.

Eddie knelt down beside her. She was so thin he could see her ribs. Her eyes were shut, but her heart was beating.

Eddie stood up and looked around. Silently he leaned over and picked up Gardenia. He carried her over to the tree where Sugar was standing. He tried to put her on the pony's back, but she was too heavy to lift so high.

He laid Gardenia down again and leaned over her. He unfastened the bag of food from the saddle. "Gardenia, I brought you some hay and some grain."

Eddie pushed some hay against the goat's mouth, but Gardenia did not open it. He held the grain to her lips, but they stayed closed.

Then Eddie ran to a puddle of rain
water. He wet his handkerchief in the
puddle and carried it back. He knelt
down again and gently opened Gardenia's
lips. Then he squeezed the water out of
his handkerchief into Gardenia's mouth.
Gardenia stuck out the tip of her tongue.
Eddie ran back to the puddle for more
water. He squeezed the water into her
mouth again. The buzzards were flapping
their great black wings overhead.

Eddie stood up and looked up at them.
"Go away! Go away!" he screamed.
"You can't have Gardenia. You can't have
her. Do you hear?"

The Walk Home

Eddie went over to the tree and unfastened Sugar. Then he leaned over and picked up Gardenia. He would have to walk home. He couldn't get on Sugar with Gardenia in his arms, and he couldn't leave her to go for help.

He followed the fence, walking slowly, holding Gardenia against his chest, and leading the pony.

Every once in a while Eddie had to sit down to rest. Gardenia was heavy even though she had grown so thin that her ribs were showing. Sugar stood and waited beside him eating grass.

Eddie finally reached the gate where he had entered the pasture. It had been a long walk, but he still had much farther to go. The sun was getting low in the west. The orange light of the late afternoon had come into the sky. He began to wonder whether he would get back to the house before dark.

He rested a few minutes before starting again after he had closed the gate. Eddie looked up. He was glad to see that the buzzards had gone. He got up and started off again. Gardenia didn't move, but Eddie could feel her heart beating against his chest. By then his legs were so tired that his feet seemed to stay in the same place.

Suddenly Eddie heard a familiar rattling and bumping. Such a rattling and bumping out here could only be the pickup truck. He looked in the direction of the sound. It was the pickup truck, and it was coming nearer and nearer. It was coming right up the road toward Eddie. In a few moments the truck had stopped beside him, and Bob stepped out.

"Eddie!" cried Bob. "What happened? What's the matter, boy?"

Bob knelt down beside Eddie. "Where did you find Gardenia?" he asked.

"Oh, Bob," cried Eddie, "she's going to be all right, isn't she? She was caught in a catclaw bush. She fell right over when I got her loose."

"Sure she's going to be all right," said Bob. "Here, let me take her, and you get in the truck."

Eddie climbed onto the seat. "I want to hold her, Bob," he said. "Don't put her in the back. I want to hold her."

"Sure," said Bob, and he laid Gardenia on Eddie's lap.

Then Bob unfastened the back of the truck and put in Sugar. He fastened the back, and in a few minutes they were on their way home.

"Now don't worry about Gardenia," said Bob. "She's going to be all right." Then Bob looked at Eddie, "You had better wipe that blood off your face and comb your hair. You'll frighten your Aunt Mary."

Eddie reached into his pocket and pulled out his wet handkerchief. He wiped his face. "I didn't scratch my face very much," said Eddie, "just my hands."

"Well, we'll fix them up with bandages when we get home," said Bob.

Soon the pickup truck stopped at the garden gate. George came running out of the house. "Hello!" he called out. When he saw Sugar in the back of the truck, he cried, "What's the matter? Why is Sugar riding in the pickup?"

Bob went around to the other side and opened the door.

"What happened?" cried George, when he saw Gardenia lying on Eddie's lap.

"She was caught in a catclaw bush," said Eddie. "But Bob said she's going to be all right, didn't you, Bob?"

"Sure did," said Bob.

226

"Did Bob get her out of the catclaw bush?" George asked.

"I should say not!" said Bob. "Eddie did it all by himself. And he's all scratched up. He needs some bandages."

Bob took Gardenia, and Eddie jumped out. His legs were so tired that they felt like rubber.

"I'll take Gardenia into the barn and make her as comfortable as possible," said Bob. "Then I'll give her some warm milk. She'll be all right. Don't worry."

When Eddie saw Aunt Mary, he couldn't possibly keep the tears back. He cried so hard that George had to tell Aunt Mary and Uncle Ed what had happened. Aunt Mary washed and wiped off Eddie's hands and arms and bound them up in a clean bandage.

"Bob," said Uncle Ed during supper, "tomorrow we'll start pulling that catclaw out of the north pasture. We don't want this to happen again."

"Yes, sir," said Bob. "We can't have that happen to Gardenia again or to any of the goats."

As soon as supper was over, Eddie went to bed. When Uncle Ed said good night, he added, "I'm proud to have a cowboy like you on my ranch."

A Present for Eddie

One morning Bob said, "I think it would be a good idea to take Gardenia back to the north pasture as soon as possible. She feels fine now, but I think she's lonely. Why don't you boys take her over this afternoon when I come back from getting the mail?"

"That's a good idea," said Eddie.

"Let's do it," said George.

When Bob returned, he had several packages in the back of the truck. Before he had a chance to take them out, Uncle Ed called him to come out to the barn.

George and Eddie came out of the house and saw the pickup truck by the gate.

"Come on," said George. "Bob's back. Let's take Gardenia over to the pasture."

"All right," said Eddie. "Let's."

The boys found Gardenia. Soon they had lifted her into the back of the truck. Uncle Ed came out and drove them to the pasture.

Uncle Ed and the boys got out. They walked around to the back of the truck, and there was Gardenia, standing in the middle of a lot of wrapping paper. Her eyes were closed in enjoyment. A piece of cardboard and streamers of wrapping paper hung from her mouth. She was quietly chewing cardboard. She had torn the paper off all the packages during the ride and had started to eat one of the cardboard boxes. At her feet lay a beautiful pair of spurs.

"Well, I'll be hanged!" said Uncle Ed. "Gardenia has opened your present, Eddie. Here are your spurs."

231

"Oh, boy!" Eddie cried in excitement as Uncle Ed handed the spurs to him.

"I sent for them the night you brought Gardenia home," said Uncle Ed. "You certainly earned them, Eddie."

Eddie sat right down on the running board of the truck and fastened the spurs to his boots. "Thanks, Uncle Ed," he said. "They're wonderful!"

Gardenia seemed pleased to be back with the other goats. She ran off and joined a group of them, torn cardboard and paper still hanging from her mouth.

Uncle Ed got back into the driver's seat, and Eddie and George climbed in beside him. As they drove away, Eddie looked back at Gardenia. Another goat was standing close beside her. He was chewing on the other end of Gardenia's piece of cardboard.

"Oh, look," Eddie exclaimed. "I'm glad Gardenia has found a friend."

The End of
the Rainbow

The Story of Tatterjack

The Scarecrow's Holiday

There is an old wives' saying that when the rainbow begins in the thorn bush and ends in the wild swan's nest, all the scarecrows in the land will come alive for one whole day.

Early one morning as the sun was shining the rain began to fall, and a great rainbow stretched across the sky. No one noticed that it rose from a thorn bush and ended where a wild swan had its nest by the river. Nor did they notice that something was happening to the scarecrow on the hill.

Old Tatterjack suddenly turned his head this way and that. He dropped his arms, and began to walk very slowly through a row in the cornfield.

The rain stopped, the sun came out, and the larks continued their songs.

"That's so much better," chuckled Tatterjack as he sat down among the flowers. He took off his torn hat to let the sun and wind play in his strawy hair.

"Why," said a voice beside him, "if it isn't old Tatterjack!"

Tatterjack turned to see Tom, the farmer's son, by his side.

"Isn't it wonderful! For one whole day I have a holiday!" cried the old fellow with enjoyment. "Oh dear, there are so many things I'd like to do. I don't know where to begin!"

The Picnic

Just then an enormous bus came around the corner and stopped. When the conductor appeared, Tom and Tatterjack realized that the bus had stopped just for them.

"Come along!" called the conductor, "we can't wait all day."

Tom and Tatterjack looked at each other and smiled. They scrambled aboard, and the bus went rolling along the road.

The bus was full of country people going to market. Some had butter and cheese or eggs and cakes to sell. One old woman had two live ducks in a basket on her lap. She sniffed and drew back her dress when the tattered old fellow with the strawy hair sat down next to her.

"Dear me," sighed the conductor. "How nice it must be to ride in the bus like a passenger. I'd rather do that than have to take money and tickets all day long."

"Please let me help you!" said Tatterjack suddenly, his old face covered with smiles.

But instead of tickets for their money, each one received one of the flowers which spilled out of Tatterjack's old pockets. Everyone thought this rather queer and smiled at the strange old fellow. They sniffed their wild flowers, and their smiles grew wider.

"How foolish we are!" said the old woman with the fat quacking ducks, "A-going to market on such a fine day!"

"Just what I was thinking, madam," said the old farmer with the cheese. "Look at the sunshine!"

The lady with the ducks made a suggestion. "Let's stop and have a picnic instead."

"Hurrah!" cried everyone, "and we'll eat our cakes, fruit, eggs, butter, and cheese by the brook!"

And believe it or not, they all stepped off the bus and began to race across the field toward the brook's edge, driver, conductor, quacking ducks, and all.

Tatterjack and Tom watched the fun until the picnic party disappeared behind the trees, then they went on their way. Tatterjack decided to spend his holiday in town even if it meant walking all the way. Tom found his friend in the tattered old clothing so gay that he decided to go with him.

The Bicycle Ride

Then Tatterjack and Tom met George, the butcher's boy, standing by his bicycle. He was looking sadly in the direction of the picnic.

"My," he said, "a picnic — and a long cool swim. Wouldn't it be fun! If only I hadn't this rackety old bicycle with me!"

"We'll ride the bicycle back to town to the butcher's shop," said Tatterjack. "Now then, Tom, get into the carrier."

And before George could nod or shake his head, Tatterjack was on the bicycle and wobbling on his way to town. As for Tom, who was squeezed into the carrier, he could only sit tight and take a deep breath as they wobbled along faster and faster.

In a short time Tatterjack and Tom reached the town. "That was wonderful," exclaimed Tatterjack.

But Tom, too out of breath to say anything, was happy to lean against a wall while Tatterjack left the bicycle outside the butcher's shop.

"Dear me!" said Tatterjack when he returned. "I have the strangest, emptiest feeling inside."

Tom knew what was wrong when he saw Tatterjack a few minutes later with his nose pushed against the window of a pie shop. His friend was hungry.

"What a beautiful smell!" said Tatterjack, sniffing outside the door. "Let's find out where it comes from."

Tatterjack Helps the Lark

One half of the shop was a restaurant. It was here that Tom found Tatterjack seated at a small table with a large piece of pie before him.

"Have some!" invited the old fellow. Tom found that he too was hungry. The woman laid a piece of juicy pie, still warm from the stove, before him.

When the pie was finished, they both sat back happily. Then the woman gave Tatterjack the bill.

"Hello!" he said, looking at the slip of paper, "What is this?"

"It's the bill," explained Tom. "What you have to pay."

"Oh dear!" said Tatterjack, "I'm afraid I haven't even a penny, madam."

Tom, who had no money either, looked at the man who owned the restaurant. Then he looked at his empty plate and wished he hadn't come to lunch with this friendly fellow.

"I'm very sorry," said Tatterjack, "but I can't pay for our lunches."

The owner looked at Tatterjack and was certainly going to be angry. Suddenly Tatterjack turned his head and rose slowly to his feet.

"Listen!" he whispered.

Everyone listened, and all at once, above the sound of dishes and the noise of traffic, a soft, sweet song was heard.

"It's Lark!" cried Tatterjack excitedly. "Last year he had a nest in my cornfield, and then — he suddenly disappeared!"

To everyone's amazement Tatterjack began to reply, very softly at first, then louder, until the restaurant was filled with the sweetest music. Everyone began to think of green fields, little streams that ran merrily across sunny pastures, wind in the tree tops, and lambs at play in the springtime.

As Tatterjack finished, everyone cheered. When Tatterjack lifted his hat, he found that the ladies and gentlemen had dropped money into it.

"Thank you," he said quickly as he counted some money to give the restaurant owner for their lunches. "Now I must find Lark."

They had to walk to the end of the street before they found Lark. When they did, Tatterjack could only stand and stare. Great tears rolled down and splashed on his nose.

Lark was sitting in a tiny cage outside the door of a small, dark shop that seemed to sell every kind of bird. There were many birds that Tom did not know, each in a cage that was much too small. But Lark appeared to be the most unhappy.

"Poor old Lark!" said Tatterjack. "Why don't you set them all free?" he asked the shopman.

"Set them free?" repeated the shopman in amazement. "Indeed, and why should I? Pay for them first, and you may do whatever you please with them afterward!"

Tatterjack put his hand deep into his pockets and brought out all the money he had left. Then he gave it to the shopman who counted it carefully.

"Why, sir," laughed the little shopman, as he finished counting, "there's only enough here for the lark and the linnet!"

"Very well, that will do."

The two unhappy birds could scarcely believe their good luck. Tatterjack and Tom opened the doors of their cages and held them high. With a song of delight they flew out, spread their wings, and went flying into the sunshine.

The birds which were left could only watch the lark and the linnet until they disappeared over the rooftops. They were so sad that they could not even sing one note.

Strangely enough, Tatterjack was not upset by the birds left behind. He smiled, and when the shopman went back into his shop, Tatterjack whistled something very softly to the birds. There was a sudden quiet, then they all began to sing and whistle together with great delight over something.

"Come along, Tom," said Tatterjack, "let's walk to the end of the next street."

A New Friend

The two friends continued their walk through the town traffic. Tom wondered what his friend was going to do next.

Tom did not have long to wait. Before they had gone very far, Tatterjack discovered that they were being followed. An old dog was keeping close to them, sniffing and barking every now and then at the foot of Tatterjack's ragged clothes. Almost at the bottom of the hill a sad cry came from behind. They turned to see the old dog seated in the middle of the street.

"Don't go any farther," his eyes seemed to say, "I'd certainly love to follow you, for you smell of fresh air and green hillsides and bushes and all the pleasant country scents that I remember. But please come with me for a moment. It's very important."

"He must be lost," said Tom. He leaned over to pat the old dog who licked his hand. "And he's so terribly thin that his ribs show."

Tatterjack once again put his hand deep into one of his pockets that seemed to hold anything from flowers to pennies. This time he brought out a great piece of bread.

250

"There you are, old fellow. That should keep you going until —"

"Until what?" repeated Tom.

"Until — well, until we find out all about who he is and where he lives."

They all went on together and the dog became more and more friendly.

"Look," said Tom, "he isn't lost at all. I'm sure he wants us to turn about and follow him."

The old dog was no longer at their heels. Instead he was trying to make his new friends follow him, which they did. After a long journey the dog led them to an address in a block of old buildings.

They climbed the stairs until they were able to look down on the rooftops of many buildings. The dog stopped at a small door in the dark hall. He barked once, wagged his tail, and then rose on his hind legs. Then very cleverly, he opened the door with his paw.

A soft voice from somewhere within invited them to enter. Tatterjack went first. There was a bed by the window, and on it lay a boy about as old as Tom. He turned in the direction of the visitors.

"Hello!" he said smiling. He was thin and pale. His hands, Tom noticed, were long and white, not at all like his own, which were strong and sunburned.

"Hello, young man," said Tatterjack. "Your dog invited us here."

"He often brings home visitors. He knows I don't mind."

"Have you been ill?" asked Tatterjack.

"Not really ill, but I was in the hospital for a long time. My legs went to sleep one day, and they forgot to wake up."

"Dear me," said Tatterjack, "and — do you live all alone?"

"Oh no, only during the day when Mother goes out to work. I'm not really lonely. There's Bob here and the birds. But on a day like this, when I can see the hills lying in the sun, it's very hard to keep still."

"I'm sure it must be," replied Tatterjack with feeling. Often he found it very hard to stand still in the middle of his cornfield and act like a scarecrow.

"How would you like to go back with us into the country, master — er —"

"Billy!" said the boy.

"— and stay there, Billy, in the sunshine?"

"For a holiday?" asked Billy.

"Well, we might call it that to begin."

"It would be wonderful!" exclaimed Billy with delight, pulling himself upright in the bed.

Tom, who had been sitting quietly saying nothing, looked at Tatterjack in amazement.

"How on earth are you going to do all that, Tatterjack?" he asked. "After all, Billy must ask his mother. She may not want to go, or she may not be able to go. And besides, where are they going to live once they get there?"

Tatterjack chuckled. "Tom, you must remember that this is no ordinary day. Anything can happen during my holiday. Now just leave everything to me. In the meantime, let's find out how we are going to take Billy and his mother into the country."

He went off in a great hurry with Tom at his heels.

Billy's eyes were shining like diamonds as he watched them go. Sometimes the doctor from the hospital was able to make him quite happy, but this merry old fellow, with the strawy hair and the wild roses spilling out of his pocket, made him want to sing.

Meantime, down in the street, Tom had to run to catch up with Tatterjack. As they walked along together, Tom kept repeating questions. Tatterjack wasn't listening though.

The Gypsy's Bargain

Across the road there was a sudden racket. A dark-haired fellow with earrings was whipping an old horse that was hitched to a gaily painted caravan. The animal had seen better days. He wobbled on his feet and looked as if he would fall down.

"Here, wait a bit!" cried Tatterjack, pushing his way through a small crowd that was beginning to gather. "What's the matter?"

The gypsy looked crossly at Tatterjack. "None of your business," he said. "If your nose didn't get in the way so much, you'd see that this good-for-nothing bag of bones had decided not to work today!" He continued to beat the frightened animal.

"Why," said Tatterjack, "you'll never make him work if you beat him."

"Do you think you could do better?"

"Of course I could do better!" replied Tatterjack. "I could teach you something about horses and start this old fellow off as quietly and easily as picking wild roses. How would you like to see him trot off like a two-year old?"

The gypsy looked at Tatterjack. His dark face plainly showed that he did not believe Tatterjack.

"See here," he said, "if you can make old Boney trot over the hill hitched to the caravan, then you may keep the whole outfit. Nothing to pay either! Now then, there's a bargain!" he cried.

He was sure that the horse was hardly fit to stand, far less run off with a caravan.

Tatterjack said nothing. His hand went into his pocket, and this time he brought out some sweet-smelling hay. The old horse began to chew it, while Tatterjack scratched him gently behind the ears. Then he whispered something to the horse. Those who were near enough to hear spent some time later telling what they had heard.

One or two said they heard a sound like the wind blowing across a field. Others were sure it was the sound of a brook spilling over rocks. Whatever the horse heard, no one ever knew, but all at once he threw back his head. A new light came into his eyes.

"Come aboard, Tom," said Tatterjack. Together they sat on the seat.

Suddenly, the old horse started forward. The wheels began to turn. This brought a cheer from the crowd.

Tatterjack did not lift the reins until the old horse swished his tail. Then the old horse put his head down and went off — at a rapid trot!

The gypsy stood with mouth wide open, while the crowd yelled and clapped. The caravan rattled over the hill.

"Well, I never!" said Tom. "Are you really going to keep the horse and caravan, Tatterjack?"

"Why not?" asked Tatterjack. "Didn't the gypsy give it to me?"

"Of course he did!" Tom agreed. "That fellow should lose both horse and caravan." Tom was wondering what his strange friend would do next.

"Tom," said Tatterjack, "please look inside the caravan and tell me what's there."

Tom disappeared inside the red door, "There's a table that folds down by the window," he called, "with a shelf on each side. One is for cups and dishes, and the other is for food. On the other side is a folding bed and a chest. At the other end of the caravan there's another bed and a rug. And there's a door at the back."

"Anything else?"

"Nothing, but a mirror — oh, and a stove with some pots and a kettle."

"Wonderful!" said Tatterjack, pulling over to the side of the road. "Now we'll go for Billy and his mother and take them into the country."

The End of a Wonderful Holiday

Billy's mother met them at the door. Tatterjack took off his hat and bowed to the pale tired woman before him.

"We're calling for you and Billy, madam," he said cheerfully. Billy's mother scarcely knew what to say to this strange old gentleman.

"Do you really mean you'd like to take Billy to the country?"

"And you, too, madam, if you'll come. Please come here for a moment," he said as he went to the window. "See, a caravan for two. You may live in it as long as you like. We know just the spot where old Bones can find food all day long, and Bob can grow young again chasing rabbits, and Billy can teach his legs to walk again!"

Tatterjack said much more. He made everything sound so wonderful that Billy's mother began to gather their belongings together and fold them into a suitcase.

"Hurrah!" cried Billy as Tatterjack led the way by carrying him downstairs.

The sun was beginning to touch the chimney tops as the caravan rattled on its way out of town. Suddenly Tatterjack stopped his horse where a crowd had gathered outside a shop.

"Sh!" he said. It seemed as if the whole street were filled with singing birds — as indeed it was!

"I can't stand it any longer," cried a familiar voice. It was the man who kept the pet store. He was letting each bird out of its cage.

"They haven't stopped screaming all afternoon. I think they've gone out of their minds since the lark and the linnet left. If I don't let the others go quickly, I'll go out of my mind too!"

Tatterjack was chuckling. "It worked, Tom," he said. "I told all the birds to sing and sing and keep on singing. And sure enough, the shopman was glad to set them free."

The shopman had just emptied the last cage. With a flapping of wings the happy flock arose from the chimney tops and flew off toward the woods. Tatterjack was smiling.

266

"What a wonderful holiday I have had!" he said as the caravan moved into the sunset.

Every morning throughout the summer, a little smoke could be seen rising from the stove in the yellow caravan in the hollow. Later, two boys would appear with an old dog at their heels. They fished near the swan's nest, or they watched an old horse eating.

But sooner or later they would turn to wave to a tall scarecrow on a hill in the distance. And Tatterjack, with the wind flapping his coat tails and a flock of crows at his feet, would throw back his head and merrily wave back.

Story Caravan

THIRD READER

New words: 359   *Total vocabulary:* 1480

Story Caravan is the third reader of the Sheldon Basic Reading Series. It is designed to be read after the successful completion of *Magic Windows*, the readiness third reader of the basic series.

Story Caravan introduces 359 new words and maintains 96% of the words taught at the previous levels of this series. Not more than 3 new words are introduced on a page.

Variant forms are not counted as new when they are formed by adding *s, es, d, ed, ing, er, est, n, en, y, ly,* or *ful* to known words. These inflectional endings include those formed by dropping the final *e*, doubling the final consonant, changing *y* to *i* or *f* to *v* before endings, and by changing *d* to *t*. Possessive forms of known words are not counted as new words. Also, not counted as new are words formed by the use of the prefixes *a* and *un*, contractions, compounds of which each part is a known word, and words which are parts of known compounds.

There will be no new words listed in poems since the reading will be a teacher-class activity.

6. Peddler's
   Timothy
   Miles
7. case
   desk
   Muley
8. Jonathan
   ornament
   Elizabeth
9. visitors
   expensive
   shelf
10. Bargain
    business
    supper
11. sold

   Ebenezer
   Plump
12. pink
    roses
    notes
13. tears
    trade
14. interested
15. . . .
16. dusty
17. leaned
    dug
    toes
18. disappeared
19. . . .
20. . . .

21. worth
22. happiness
    pay
    washed
23. . . .
24. . . .
25. Betty
    dishes
    sight
26. President
    Washington
    coach
27. parents
    George
    butter
28. April

268

29. porch
30. pretty
    spread
    cloth
31. kissed
    cellar
    forehead
32. sneeze
    shoulder
33. log
    British
    bushes
34. Becky
    sail
35. hid
36. lying
    shirt
    tattered
37. . . .
38. sewed
    shut
39. scouting
    lad
40. untruth
    lie
    protection
41. spinning
    terrible
42. . . .
43. . . .
44. . . .
45. prince
    princess
    marry
46. lightning
    goodness
    heels
47. pea
    twenty
    mattresses
48. least
49. purple
    Marlaine
    castle
50. order
    impossible
51. indeed

sent
nodded
52. promised
    reward
53. dye
    Nell
    color
54. stared
55. . . .
56. . . .
57. notice
    fooled
58. choose
59. . . .
60. James
    John
61. winks
    twice
    earth
62. dwarf
    deed
63. diamonds
64. toothpicks
    rusty
65. thrown
66. flapping
    wings
    rich
67. . . .
68. half
69. . . .
70. arrive
71. sharp
    died
    fearful
72.
73. lips
74. . . .
75. . . .
76. crown
    mountain
77. . . .
78. valentines
    Anya
    Mama
79. empty
80. Riggs

calendar
February
81. Frank
82. disappointed
83. poured
    decorated
    none
84. wrappings
    dessert
    neat
85. chocolate
    baked
    upstairs
86. . . .
87. . . .
88. . . .
89. giraffe
    camera
    Archie
90. projector
    bother
91. jokes
92. lesson
    beast
93. Africa
94. . . .
95. . . .
96. forty
97. true
98. cost
    thirty
    hundred
99. . . .
100. . . .
101. . . .
102. . . .
103. . . .
104. smart
105. scream
106. announcer
    Easter
    sunrise
107. husband
108. sweep
    mending
109. polite
110. deliver

269

111. . . .
112. fifth
113. clever
114. . . .
115. lake
116. trip
117. yet
118. . . .
119. . . .
120. . . .
121. . . .
122. . . .
123. . . .
124. Crumpet
London
Preparations
125. Professor
Beep
realized
126. huge
inventor
explorer
127. Coronation
rather
madam
128. services
recognize
charge
129. Bouncing
drew
kangaroo
130. weeping
failed
131. bounded
scarcely
132. bit
South
133. escape
pot
mixture
134. . . .
135. less
measure
distance
136. . . .
137. tighten

lap
strap
138. clothing
discovered
139. banner
balloons
immediately
140. rows
rent
141. flags
loose
142. . . .
143. . . .
144. Daniel's
Henry
Boarder
145. Wanda
146. playmate
doctor
months
147. fit
pale
148. wrote
pages
stray
149. Ada
Albert
Beulah
150. . . .
151. Lucy
tip
whose
152. intelligent
chance
153. silence
154. spanking
suggestions
155. agreed
mind
meant
156. chained
nervous
157. knelt
hay
158. . . .
159. begged
160. millstone

afford
lazy
161. weeds
tusks
162. sank
rapidly
scrambled
163. . . .
164. . . .
165. . . .
166. state
167. Kristen
Kippie
goat
168. . . .
169. cane
170. attention
tap
171. disobeyed
172. pipe
stamped
173. edge
Trolley
curious
174. entered
comfortable
175. passengers
176. office
rule
177. traffic
arrested
178. restaurant
179. refused
Famous
foolish
180. though
181. fifty
cups
fifteen
182. fellow
prize
183. third
carrot
whip
184. stubborn
185. earned
186. . . .

270

187. . . .
188. Silently
189. . . .
190. . . .
191. . . .
192. Gardenia
    Eddie
    Wilson
193. chewing
    canvas
    enjoyment
194. Edward
    automobile
195. . . .
196. . . .
197. collar
198. comb
    throat
199. continued
200. Texas
201. address
202. received
    hall
    cousin
203. spend
204. . . .
205. baggage
    spurs
206. suitcase
    grain
207. . . .
208. excitement
209. porter
    streamlined
210. . . .
211. button
    aboard
212. . . .
213. saddle

    north
    pasture
214. west
    Buzzards
    reins
215. thick
216. . . .
217. thorns
    Catclaw
    beat
218. blood
    fur
    ribs
219. unfastened
220. puddle
    handkerchief
    squeezed
221. chest
222. . . .
223. direction
    matter
224. . . .
225. bandages
    wipe
226. . . .
227. possible
228. during
229. . . .
230. . . .
231. cardboard
    torn
232. . . .
233. . . .
234. Swans
    Scarecrows
    Holiday
235. larks
    chuckled
    strawy

236. . . .
237. cheese
238. spilled
239. brooks
240. Bicycle
    butcher's
    wobbling
241. pie
242. invited
    stove
243. . . .
244. . . .
245. counted
    amazement
246. . . .
247. repeated
    delight
    linnet
248. . . .
249. . . .
250. . . .
251. . . .
252. . . .
253. . . .
254. . . .
255. . . .
256. . . .
257. Gypsy's
    caravan
258. . . .
259. . . .
260. . . .
261. . . .
262. folds
263. . . .
264. . . .
265. . . .
266. . . .
267. . . .

Acknowledgments

Grateful acknowledgment is made to the following for permission to use and adapt copyrighted materials:

Blackie and Son, Ltd. for "The Story of Tatterjack" from *The Story of Tatterjack* by Gregor Ian Smith, reprinted by permission of the publishers.

Beatrice Curtis Brown for "Jonathan Bing" from *Jonathan Bing and Other Verses* by Beatrice Curtis Brown. Copyright 1936 by the author, reprinted by permission of the author.

Child Life Magazine for "The Saving Sneeze" from *The Saving Sneeze* by Lenore M. McCulloch. Copyright 1953, used by permission of the author and the publishers.

B. J. Chute for "Archie and the April Fools" adapted from *Archie and the April Fools* from Child Life Magazine. Copyright 1942, used by permission of the author and the publishers.

Harcourt, Brace and Company, Inc. for "James the Huntsman" from *Thirteen Danish Tales* retold by Mary C. Hatch. Copyright 1947, used by permission of the publishers.

D. C. Heath and Company for "The Little Cook" from *Old Times Stories of the North State* by Lutie A. McCorkle, reprinted by permission of the publishers.

The McBride Company, Inc. for "Otherwise" from *Coffee Pot Face* by Aileen Fisher, by permission of the publishers.

Julian Messner, Inc. for "Kippie the Cow" from *Kippie the Cow* by Esther Gretor. Copyright October 22, 1951, by permission of the publishers.

Harold Ober Associates for "The Country Bunny and the Little Gold Shoes" from *The Country Bunny and the Little Gold Shoes* by Marjorie Flack and DuBose Heyward. Copyright 1939 by the authors.

Story Parade, Inc. for "The Peddler's Clock" by Mabel Leigh Hunt, copyright 1936; "Valentines for America" by Mildred Lawrence, copyright 1953; "Miss Crumpet's Great Day" by Frank Rosengren, copyright 1938; "Daniel's Elephant" from *Daniel Webster's Elephant* by Jack Bechdolt, copyright 1950. All reprinted by permission of the publishers.